# DEEP DIVE

## DEVOTIONS FOR FAMILIES

### Learning More About God and His Love for Us

Daniel Carr, Brad Delaughter & Martin Winslow

high
street
press

# Acknowledgments

The authors and staff of High Street Press wish to thank the following people for their contributions to this book:

Executive editor: John Yeats
Editors: Gary Ledbetter & Rob Phillips
Cover design: Allen Sutton
Layout: Allen Sutton
Production management: Gary Ledbetter
Electronic production: Tony Boes
Scripture verification: Jill Campbell
Proofreading: Nancy Phillips

High Street Press is the publishing arm of the Missouri Baptist Convention (MBC) and exists because of the generous support of Missouri Baptists through the Cooperative Program.

To learn more about the MBC and the way 1,750 affiliated churches cooperate voluntarily for the sake of the gospel, visit **mobaptist.org**.

To learn more about High Street Press, go online to **highstreet.press**.

# Contents

# PART 1 | Who Is God?

By Martin Winslow

A knock came at my door. When I answered, I met two people inviting me to their church. I quickly understood that they worshiped a different God than I do. They were Jehovah's Witnesses.

They began to explain how the Christian church had been deceived early in its history and that I, and everyone who went to church with me, worshiped a false god. They told me that Jesus is not God and that he never claimed to be God. They also said the Holy Spirit is just a force; he is not a person, and he is definitely not God.

Many Christians have had this experience, and many are not ready to answer with the truth. Even though the doctrine of God can be hard to explain, it's important for us to know and confidently tell others what we believe about God. Once you spend time studying the subject, it becomes easier to understand the basics and talk about them to others. My hope is that this book gives you and your family insight into who God has revealed himself to be in Scripture.

For a human to fully explain how the nature of God works is like your dog or cat explaining how the engine in your car works. Fortunately, Christians have the Scriptures to lean on when it comes to knowing more about the Lord. God has revealed himself to be the only God in the universe. He is the only one who is, and ever will be, God.

Isaiah 43:10 reads, "'You are My witnesses' — this is the LORD'S declaration — 'and My servant whom I have chosen, so that you may know and believe Me and understand that I am He. No god was formed before Me, and there will be none after Me.'"

Yet, we also see that God's nature is plural. How can God be one and three at the same time? We don't exactly understand, but we can see this is what Scripture clearly teaches and believe it. In this book, you will learn what Scripture teaches about God, and about the background debates that took place in the early church. The early church didn't invent the Trinity. "Trinity" is a word used to explain what we see in the Scriptures.

As one author puts it, "Are there more gods than one? There is only one God. In how many persons does this one God exist? In three persons. Who are they? The Father, the Son, and the Holy Spirit."[1]

This book is designed in small chapters geared toward helping families understand who the God of the Bible has revealed himself to be. I recommend that parents read one chapter a night with their kids and talk through the "Questions to consider" and "Truths to remember."

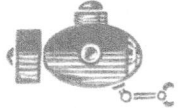

# PART 1.1 | What/Who is the Trinity?

MEMORY VERSE - DEUT. 6:4
"Listen, Israel: The LORD our God, the LORD is One."

## Trinity

The word "Trinity" comes from two words. The first is "tri," meaning "three," and the second is "unity," meaning "together" or "unified." When we speak of the Trinity, we are speaking of the three persons – Father, Son, and Holy Spirit – who make up the one eternal God we worship as Christians. Tertullian, an early church father, was the first to use the word Trinity when explaining the nature of God. The word is not in the Bible, but rather is used to explain what we observe by reading the Bible.

Romans 11:33 reminds us of the majesty of the great God of the universe: "How unsearchable His judgments and untraceable His ways!" For us to think that we can understand everything about the infinite God is arrogant. What we can do is look at what he has revealed about himself and accept it as true, even if we don't understand all of it.

God is triune. God is three distinct persons, yet only one God. To say he is three and he is one may seem like doublespeak, but it's the clear teaching of the Old and New Testaments. James White says that a discussion of the Trinity needs to start with a short, succinct definition of what we mean by "Trinity." He writes, "Within the one Being that is God, there exists eternally three coequal and coeternal persons, namely, the Father, the Son, and the Holy Spirit."[2]

## One being that is God

White begins by saying there is "one Being that is God." Deuteronomy 6:4 clearly sets forth this truth about the Hebrew God. This passage is called the "Shema" and was recited each day by the Hebrew people. It says, "Listen, Israel: The LORD our God, the LORD is One."

When we get to the New Testament, we find this same truth repeated several times. When Jesus is asked to name the greatest commandment (Mark 12:29), he answers by quoting Deuteronomy 6:4. Paul affirms this important teaching in 1 Timothy 2:5. Numerous other passages could be cited to demonstrate that there is only one God according to the Scriptures. But it's also very important to realize that each of the three persons who make up the one God are equal and distinct.

# Coequal and coeternal

We also see the coequal and coeternal plurality that exists within the Godhead. "Coequal" means each person is equal to the others. "Coeternal" means none of the persons of the Trinity ever had a beginning. They are, each and all, eternal.

In Genesis 1:1, the word for God, "Elohim," is in a plural form. The grammar forces a singular translation of the word "God," yet, in form, the word is plural. When God creates, he goes on to say, "Let Us make man in Our image" (Gen. 1:26). If God refers to himself as "us," it is implied that the three persons are equal.

We also realize that God refers to himself in the plural from the very beginning. A close reading of the Bible demonstrates that all three persons are present in the creation account. The Father speaks, and by his spoken word, the world is made. John 1:1 tells us, "In the beginning was the Word, and the Word was with God, and the Word was God." Verse 14 identifies the Word as Jesus. Jesus is the Word of God who creates in Genesis 1.

We also see in Genesis 1:2 that "the Spirit of God was hovering over the surface of the waters." All three persons can be seen in the creation account: Father, Son, and Holy Spirit. That the Spirit and Son must be God is affirmed when God speaks in Isaiah, "I am Yahweh, who made everything; who stretched out the heavens by Myself; who alone spread out the earth" (Isa. 44:24).

If God claims to be all alone in the creation, yet the Spirit and the Son are clearly seen creating, then the logical conclusion is that the Father, Son, and Holy Spirit are all the one God, making them not only coequal, but coeternal.

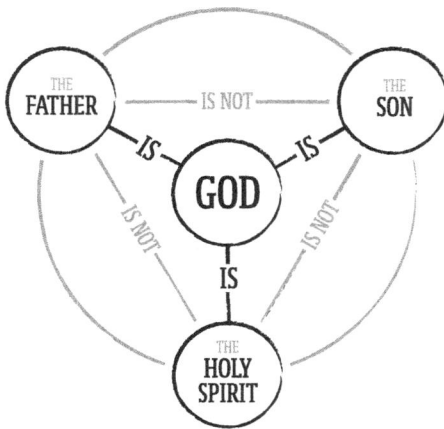

Notice the picture above.[3] God is "one" in the middle. Branching out from the middle in three different directions is the word "is." God is Father, he is Son, and he is the Holy Spirit. The lines that connect the three persons on the outside all say, "is not." The Father is not the Son or the Holy Spirit. Each person is distinct.

At Jesus' baptism we see that the persons of the Trinity are distinct from one another. Mark 1:9-11 says:

> In those days Jesus came from Nazareth in Galilee and was baptized in the Jordan by John. As soon as He came up out of the water, He saw the heavens being torn open and the Spirit descending to Him like a dove. And a voice came from heaven: "You are My beloved Son; I take delight in You!"

Notice that the Spirit descended like a dove as Jesus came up out of the waters of baptism. Then the voice of the Father called Jesus his Son. Clearly, each person is distinct. Jesus also, on many occasions, prays to his Father in the New Testament (Matt. 14:23; Luke 5:16; John 17). Jesus also says the Holy Spirit will be sent to the church: "The Counselor, the Holy Spirit — the Father will send Him in My name" (John 14:26). Jesus and the Father weren't sending themselves; they were sending another – namely, the Holy Spirit. Yet, don't forget that each person is fully God, and they are one God.

Don't think of God like this: $1 + 1 + 1 = 3$. Think of God according to higher math: $1 \times 1 \times 1 = 1$.

# God is not like me (a son, a brother, and a father)

Sometimes, people try to explain the Trinity with illustrations. I have heard people say, "God is like me. I am a son, a brother, and a father all at one time, yet I am just one guy." The problem with this is that God is simultaneously three distinct persons as we see in Christ's baptism. God is not like one man playing three different roles at the same time. In Christ's baptism, we see the Son coming up out of the water, the Spirit descending like a dove, and the voice of the Father from heaven. God is three persons!

# Questions to consider

1. What does the word "Trinity" mean?

2. Are the Father, Son, and Holy Spirit the same person?

3. How many Gods are there?

4. What if someone, talking about the Trinity, says to you, "1 + 1 + 1 = 3... the math doesn't add up"?

# Truths to remember

1. God is not like me. He is not one person who plays three different roles.

2. There is only one God. He is three persons, and we can see these three persons distinctly at the baptism of Jesus (Mark 1:9-11).

3. Each person of the Trinity is coequal and coeternal with the other persons.

# PART 1.2 | God Is One, God Is Three

MEMORY VERSE - MATT. 28:19

"Go, therefore, and make disciples of all nations, baptizing them in the name of the Father and of the Son and of the Holy Spirit."

Notice that the Scripture passage above says we are to baptize in the name of the Father, Son, and Holy Spirit. Isn't it interesting how the word "name" is in the singular? Wouldn't proper grammar say, "the *names* of the Father and the Son and the Holy Spirit"? Since there is only one God, the word "name" remains singular.

Since God is at the same time three persons, each person – Father, Son, and Holy Spirit – is mentioned. We can see in this baptismal formula that Jesus gave a perfect reflection of the nature of God – one God in three persons! The early church struggled to understand God as three persons and, at the same time, one God.

## Jesus is God: The Council of Nicaea

In the fourth century, an intense debate began within the Roman Empire over the question of whether Jesus is a created being. The true Christian tradition held that Jesus is as fully God as God the Father. Tradition also taught that the Holy Spirit is fully God, yet there is only one God.

Enter Arius, a preacher from Alexandria who taught that Jesus is not actually God. On the other side of the argument, the scriptural position declared that the Father, Son, and Holy Spirit are three persons of the one God. This debate grew intense within the church.

Finally, Emperor Constantine called for a council to meet in Nicaea to resolve the issue. Around three hundred bishops from different parts of the empire came to Nicaea to resolve this important question over the nature of God. Was Arius right, and Jesus is less than God? Or, were the Trinitarians correct in claiming that God is three fully divine persons?

One of the bishops who came to these debates in Nicaea was the bishop of Myra. His name was Nicholas. Nicholas was a kind and loving bishop we know today as St. Nick. The modern tradition of Santa Claus is built on the shoulders of this generous man. Nicholas was a Trinitarian and believed Arius was teaching false ideas and hurting the church. At one point during the debate, Nicholas punched Arius for his false teaching. The real "Santa Claus" was a defender of the truth about Jesus Christ!

Below is the Creed of Nicaea. "Creed," or credo, is the first Latin word in this statement and means "I believe." The bishops in Nicaea signed their names to this document, declaring that the Father, Son, and Holy Spirit are each fully God, yet there is one God. It's important to note, when we approach the difficult subject of God, that each person of the Trinity shares completely and fully in the being that is God.

James White, in *The Forgotten Trinity*, writes:

> ... the Father is not 1/3 of God, the Son 1/3 of God, the Spirit 1/3 of God. Each is fully God, coequal with the others, and that eternally. There never was a time when the Father was not the Father; never a time when the Son was not the Son; never a time when the Spirit was not the Spirit.[4]

Following is the Nicene Creed, developed by the bishops at the Council of Nicaea. This creed is a statement of belief by the early church on what they believe the Scriptures teach about the nature of God.

# The Nicene Creed

> *I believe in one God, the Father Almighty,* Maker of heaven and earth, and of all things visible and invisible, and *in one Lord Jesus Christ,* the only-begotten Son of God, begotten of the Father before all worlds; God of God, Light of Light, very God of very God; begotten, not made, being of one substance with the Father, by whom all things were made ...
>
> Who, for us men and for our salvation, came down from heaven, and was incarnate by the Holy Spirit of the virgin Mary, and was made man; and was crucified also for us under Pontius Pilate; He suffered and was buried; and the third day He rose again, according to the Scriptures; and ascended into

heaven, and sits on the right hand of the Father; and He shall come again, with glory, to judge the quick and the dead; whose kingdom shall have no end.

And *I believe in the Holy Spirit, the Lord and Giver of Life;* who proceeds from the Father and the Son; who with the Father and the Son together is worshiped and glorified; who spoke by the prophets.

And I believe in one holy catholic and apostolic Church. I acknowledge one baptism for the remission of sins; and I look for the resurrection of the dead, and the life of the world to come. Amen.[5]

I emphasized in the creed that the belief of the early church bishops was "One God," who is "the Father Almighty, Maker of heaven and earth." I also emphasized "one Lord Jesus Christ," and the creed says of him that he is "God of God." The Holy Spirit is then called "the Lord and Giver of Life." The bishops based all these statements on the clear teaching of Scripture. I will elaborate more on this in the chapters that follow.

# Who raised Jesus from the dead?

One way to understand that God is one and God is three is by answering the question, "Who raised Jesus from the dead?"

The Book of Acts tells the history of the early church and how churches were planted as the gospel spread. The main thrust of the teaching of the early church was that God raised Jesus. In Acts 2:32, Peter says, "God has resurrected this Jesus. We are all witnesses of this ...." Later, in Acts 10:40, Peter, while preaching to a man named Cornelius, says, "God raised up this man on the third day and permitted Him to be seen ...."

Later, in Acts 17:30-31, Paul writes:
> Therefore, having overlooked the times of ignorance, God now commands all people everywhere to repent, because He has set a day when He is going to judge the world in righteousness by the Man He has appointed. He has provided proof of this to everyone by raising Him from the dead.

These passages show that the teaching of the early church was that God alone is the one who raised Jesus. The Scripture goes on to indicate that each person of the Trinity was active in raising Jesus.

Galatians 1:1 tells us the Father raised Jesus: "Paul, an apostle — (not from men or by man, but by Jesus Christ and God the Father who raised Him from the dead) ...."

Yet, Jesus predicts raising himself from the dead: "Jesus answered, 'Destroy this sanctuary, and I will raise it up in three days.' Therefore the Jews said, 'This sanctuary took 46 years to build, and will You raise it up in three days?' But He was speaking about the sanctuary of His body" (John. 2:19-21).

Then, Paul tells us that the Holy Spirit raised Jesus from the dead: "And if the Spirit of Him who raised Jesus from the dead lives in you, then He who raised Christ from the dead will also bring your mortal bodies to life through His Spirit who lives in you" (Rom. 8:11).

These passages of Scripture, taken together, show us that God is one God in three persons.

# Questions to consider

1. Why is it significant that Jesus commands his disciples to baptize in the singular name of the Father, Son, and Holy Spirit?

2. What famous person was at the Council of Nicaea? What happened between him and Arius?

3. What does the word "creed" mean?

# Truths to remember

1. The three persons aren't each one-third of God. Each is fully God, yet God is one.

2. The early church statement at Nicaea helped guide the church on the nature of God.

3. The early preaching of the church was that God raised Jesus from the dead. We also see in the New Testament that each person of the Godhead is said to have raised Jesus.

# PART 1.3 | God Is Father

MEMORY VERSES - EPH. 4:4-6
"There is one body and one Spirit — just as you were called to one hope at your calling — one Lord, one faith, one baptism, one God and Father of all, who is above all and through all and in all."

## God is our heavenly Father

Each child has physical needs that parents must meet for the child to thrive. Parents must provide for their children's health needs. They feed them, care for them, and nurture them as they grow. Our heavenly Father provides for us every moment of every day. The air we breathe, the sun that keeps us warm, and the rain that waters the flowers are all because God is a father to us.

Psalm 19:1-4 illustrates how our heavenly Father takes care of us and speaks to us:

> The heavens declare the glory of God, and the sky proclaims the work of His hands. Day after day they pour out speech; night after night they communicate knowledge. There is no speech; there are no words; their voice is not heard. Their message has gone out to all the earth, and their words to the ends of the world.

God the Father has spoken to us by caring for us and speaking to us in his created universe. God's loving acts of meeting our daily needs through sustaining the universe demonstrates his fatherly care for us. God's kindness as Father can also be seen in his loving care for those who are vulnerable and needy.

Psalm 68:5 says, "God in His holy dwelling is a father of the fatherless and a champion of widows." God cares for the widow and the orphan! He is truly a kind Father. In the Gospels, Jesus refers to God the Father 165 times.

# What do we mean by the "first, second, and third" persons of the Trinity?

If you were competing in a race and crossed the finish line in second or third place, you might be disappointed that you didn't win. It may seem in calling Jesus the "second" person of the Trinity, or the Holy Spirit the "third" person of the Trinity, we are implying they are less than God the Father, the first person of the Trinity. This isn't true at all.

When we refer to the first, second, and third persons of the Godhead, we are speaking of the order in which God revealed his personhood to us. Though, we can see hints of God's triune nature in Genesis 1:26 when he says, "Let Us make man in Our image ...."

We don't clearly see God the Son until the birth of Jesus in Bethlehem. We find out from the Gospel of John that this baby born in Bethlehem is also the creator of the world (John 1:1-3, 14). God the Father sent God the Son. The Son was the second person of the Trinity to be revealed to us.

We also see hints of the Holy Spirit's work in creation as the Spirit of God moves over the surface of the water in Genesis 1:2. However, it's not until Jesus tells us more about the Spirit's work (John 14-16), and then the Spirit reveals himself to the church in Acts 2, that we see the Holy Spirit in his fullness. He (The Spirit) is the third person of the Trinity to be revealed to us.

# The relationship within the Trinity

Is one of the persons of the Godhead more powerful than the others? Who's in charge? In John 14:28, Jesus says, "The Father is greater than I." If Jesus is God, the question might be raised, "How can someone be greater than God?" The answer to this question is actually simple. While Jesus does claim that the Father is greater than he is, he never says the Father is *better* than he is. "Greater" refers to office, while "better" refers to nature.

There are a couple of easy examples of this, drawn from everyday life. The President of the United States is greater than any other American.

He holds an office that supersedes any other office in the U.S. While this is true, it's also true that the President of the United States is not better than any other American. He's just a man and shares the same nature that all men share. He is no better than anyone else.

Jesus is speaking of his office in relationship to the Father. The second person of the Trinity, while being the Father's equal in nature, is still the one who humbled himself in the Incarnation. He (Jesus) assumed the role of a servant.

Another example of greater not meaning better can be seen in the way God has set up the marriage relationship between a man and a woman. A wife is to be submissive to her husband. The husband is the head of the house (Eph. 5:23). However, the man is never said to be better than his wife. He simply has a role greater than that of his wife.

Within the Godhead, we see this same kind of submissiveness. It's perfectly sensible that Jesus could say, "The Father is greater than I." There is no contradiction in this truth and the truth that Jesus is fully God.

# Our Father who is in heaven

Jesus invites his disciples to call God "Father." In Matthew's Gospel, Jesus teaches his disciples how to pray. He says, "Therefore, you should pray like this: Our Father in heaven, Your name be honored as holy" (Matt. 6:9). "Holy" means "set apart," yet Jesus tells us we can call on him as Father.

1 John 3:1 says, "Look at how great a love the Father has given us that we should be called God's children. And we are!" God loves you and invites you to have a relationship with him. It's amazing that Jesus tells us we can call God "Father." When you pray, call out to your heavenly Father with your requests.

Jesus says in Matthew 7:9-11:

> What man among you, if his son asks him for bread, will give him a stone? Or if he asks for a fish, will give him a snake? If you then, who are evil, know how to give good gifts to your children, how much more will your Father in heaven give good things to those who ask Him!

You exist to have a relationship with God. If an earthly father will take care of your needs, how much more will our heavenly Father?

As Paul writes: "Yet for us there is one God, the Father. All things are from Him, and we exist for Him. And there is one Lord, Jesus Christ. All things are through Him, and we exist through Him" (I Cor. 8:6).

# Questions to consider

1. What are some basic ways God shows himself to be like a father in creation?

2. What two types of vulnerable people does God take care of according to Psalm 68:5?

3. If God the Father is the first person of the Trinity, does that mean he is more important than the Son or Holy Spirit?

4. Is it okay to refer to God as "Father" in our prayers?

# Truths to remember

1. God's lovingkindness can be seen through his provision each day in creation.

2. Jesus refers to God as Father 165 times in the New Testament.

3. "Greater" does not mean "better." When Jesus says the Father is greater than he is, he's only speaking about the Father's position in relation to the Son, not that the Father's value is higher than the Son's. The President of the United States is greater than I am, but not better.

# PART 1.4 | God Is Son

### MEMORY VERSES - JOHN 1:1-3

"In the beginning was the Word, and the Word was with God, and the Word was God. He was with God in the beginning. All things were created through Him, and apart from Him not one thing was created that has been created."

## The deity of Christ

Pastor and author A. W. Tozer once said, "What comes to our minds when we think about God is the most important thing about us."[6] We must do our best to understand and teach the truth about God. When we look at the New Testament, the deity of Christ (the fact that he is God) is evident, even at a surface reading.

John's Gospel is a simple place to start when understanding that Jesus is God in the flesh. Modern-day Jehovah's Witnesses hold the same position that Arius of Alexandria held during the Council of Nicaea. The view of Arius that Jesus was a created being was rejected at Nicaea and by the early church.

When Jehovah's Witnesses come to your door, you might direct them to John 1:1-3. They claim that John 1:1 should read, "the Word [Jesus] was *a* god" and not the one true God. The context, however, demonstrates the weakness of their translation (The New World Translation). If you keep reading the next two verses, Jesus is proclaimed the one true creator.

Those verses say, "All things were created through Him, and apart from Him not one thing was created that has been created." If nothing has come to be that he didn't make, how can Jesus be a created being? He made everything. In the original Greek, it says there is not even "one single" thing he didn't make.

John 1:1-3 is clearly teaching that Jesus is God, because God said he was by himself when he created. In Isaiah 44:24, God says that he "stretched out the heavens by Myself; who alone spread out the earth." If God did this by himself, and Jesus created any of God's creation, it would be understood, according to John 1:1-3, that Jesus is God.

Another great passage to show Jehovah's Witnesses that Jesus is God is John 8:58. In this passage, Jesus claims to be the one true God. He tells the Pharisees, "I assure you: Before Abraham was, I AM." In Exodus 3:14, God reveals himself to Moses as the I AM. When Jesus uses this same phrase to identify himself, his audience picks up stones to kill him. Why did they want to kill him for saying this? Because he was making himself equal with God.

# Jesus is worshiped!

Another great way to prove the Scriptures teach that Jesus is God is by examining who alone can be worshiped. When Satan tempts Jesus in Matthew 4:10, the devil says to Jesus, "'I will give You all these things if You will fall down and worship me.' Then Jesus told him, 'Go away, Satan! For it is written: Worship the Lord your God, and serve only Him.'"

By Jesus' own mouth, he declares that worship is reserved for God. Does Jesus' statement imply in any way that he is not God? In fact, when we look at the rest of the New Testament, we see that Jesus is worshiped by his disciples.

Jehovah's Witnesses say that Jesus is the archangel Michael, yet Hebrews 1:5 asks an important question: "For to which of the angels did He ever say, 'You are My Son; today I have become Your Father, or again, I will be His Father, and He will be My Son?'" The answer is that God has said this to none of his angels.

Hebrews 1:6 goes on to say, "When He again brings His firstborn into the world, He says, 'And all God's angels must worship Him.'" Remember Matthew 4:10? It says that worship is only for God, yet the Father has the Son worshiped by his angels in this passage.

Hebrews 1:5-8 disproves the idea that Jesus was an angel, and that Jesus isn't worshiped as God. The very last verse of Revelation 5 has every created thing falling down before the Lamb (Jesus) and worshiping.

Another good passage to prove this important point comes after the resurrection of Jesus, when he visits his disciples. In Matthew 28:9, Jesus is being worshiped, with his disciples holding his feet. In verse 17, it happens again. Jesus never rebukes his disciples for worshiping him. If he were merely a created angel, he would have rebuked them, as the angel in Revelation 19:20 rebuked John when he tried to worship him.

Jesus is not an angel. He is the creator of angels and everything else in the universe. We must worship and adore him as our creator God (Phil. 2:11).

Charles Wesley wrote a beautiful song called "Hark the Herald Angels Sing." In verse 2, the following is sung:

> Christ, by highest heav'n adored;
> Christ the everlasting Lord;
> Late in time, behold Him come,
> Offspring of a virgin's womb.
> Veiled in flesh the Godhead see;
> Hail th'incarnate Deity,
> Pleased with us in flesh to dwell,
> Jesus our Emmanuel.

# Jesus is one of a kind

Another church council was convened in AD 451 to discuss the scriptural teaching regarding the dual nature of Christ, that he was both God and man. This council was held in Chalcedon. The council's verdict upheld the scriptural teaching that Christ was fully God and fully human.

Even though Christ had a human nature and divine nature, Christ was one person, not two. Somehow, when God became a man in the person of Jesus, he remained what he was (God) and became what he was not (human). Jesus is the God-Man. There is no one like Jesus.

The Scriptures teach that both natures of humanity and deity could be clearly seen during the life of Jesus. Jesus said, "I'm thirsty" (John 19:28). He also ate with his disciples (Matt. 14:12-25). Does God get hungry or thirsty? He does not. The man Jesus did get hungry and thirsty.

The Scriptures also tell us that Jesus is the creator of everything (John 1:1-3) and raised himself from the dead (John 2:19-21). Could a man create the universe or raise himself from the dead? He could not. Jesus is truly one of a kind.

Because of his unique nature as both God and man, Jesus became the perfect sacrifice for mankind. Only God is pure, holy, and good.

Jesus meets these qualifications. The Bible also tells us that "without the shedding of blood there is no forgiveness" (Heb. 9:22). Because Jesus was a perfect human, he was able to die for the sins of the world (Heb. 10:12; 1 John 2:2).

In the Book of Acts, Paul teaches the Ephesian elders, "Be on guard for yourselves and for all the flock, among which the Holy Spirit has made you overseers, to shepherd the church of God which He purchased with His own blood" (Acts 20:28). Who does Paul say purchased the church with his own blood? God.

## Questions to consider

1. How do we know, using John 1:3, that John 1:1-2 teaches that Jesus is God?

2. How are John 8:58 and Exodus 3:14 similar passages of Scripture? What is Jesus saying about himself by quoting from Exodus?

3. What does Matthew 4:10 say? Why is that verse important in light of Matthew 28:9?

4. Since Jesus is fully God and fully man, does this make him two persons instead of one?

## Truths to remember

1. Christ is the creator, as John 1:1-3 says. John 1:14 says, "the Word became flesh and dwelt among us." Jesus is the Word who was in the beginning.

2. Jesus is worshiped on several occasions in the New Testament; yet, by Jesus' own teaching, only God is to be worshiped (Matt. 4:10).

3. In no passage of Scripture where Jesus is worshiped does he refuse it.

4. Jesus is unique in that he is, simultaneously, fully God and fully man.

# PART 1.5 | God Is Holy Spirit

MEMORY VERSE - 2 COR. 3:17
"Now the Lord is the Spirit, and where the Spirit of the Lord is, there is freedom."

## The Holy Spirit is God

James White says, "There is a reason why the Holy Spirit does not receive the same level and kind of attention that is focused upon the Father and the Son: it is not His purpose to attract that kind of attention to Himself."[7] White is correct; in fact, Jesus himself said of the Spirit, "He will glorify Me, because He will take from what is Mine and declare it to you" (John 16:14).

The Holy Spirit was sent from the Father "to convict the world about sin, righteousness, and judgment" (John 16:8). The Spirit leads people to Christ. Christ is the one who died for the sins of the world. Christ is the one through whom we may, by faith, have a relationship with God. The Holy Spirit is the one who nudges our hearts when we hear the Word of God. He's the one who brings upon us conviction that leads to belief in the gospel. The Holy Spirit nudges us toward Jesus.

What passages of Scripture teach that the Holy Spirit is God? We see that the Spirit was involved in the creation of the world (Gen. 1:2). We also see that Job believed the Holy Spirit created him as well. Job says, "The Spirit of God has made me, and the breath of the Almighty gives me life" (Job 33:4). The Spirit is also omnipresent (everywhere at once). Psalm 139:7 says, "Where can I go to escape Your Spirit? Where can I flee from Your presence?" The answer to this, obviously, is "nowhere."

The Spirit also is all-knowing. In 1 Corinthians 2:10-11, we read:

> Now God has revealed these things to us by the Spirit, for the Spirit searches everything, even the depths of God. For who among men knows the thoughts of a man except the spirit of the man that is in him? In the same way, no one knows the thoughts of God except the Spirit of God.

Other Old Testament passages clearly indicate that when the Holy Spirit speaks, he is speaking the words of God (1 Sam. 10:10; Zech. 7:12).

# The Holy Spirit is not a force

The Holy Spirit is not a force, as some make him out to be. He is a personal being, and we should talk about him as a real person. A force cannot speak or send someone to do something, as we see the Holy Spirit do in Acts 13:2. This passage says, "the Holy Spirit said, 'Set apart for Me Barnabas and Saul for the work I have called them to.'" The passage goes on to say, "Being sent out by the Holy Spirit, they came down to Seleucia" (v. 4). The Holy Spirit both speaks and sends in this passage.

In Hebrews 10:15-17, we again see that the Holy Spirit speaks: "The Holy Spirit also testifies to us about this. For after He says: 'This is the covenant I will make with them after those days, says the Lord: I will put My laws on their hearts and write them on their minds, He adds: I will never again remember their sins and their lawless acts.'"

A force cannot speak, yet we see speech from the Holy Spirit. He must be a person. The Holy Spirit also speaks for us when we don't know what to say in our prayers. Romans 8:26 says, "In the same way the Spirit also joins to help in our weakness, because we do not know what to pray for as we should, but the Spirit Himself intercedes for us with unspoken groanings." Isn't it amazing to know that if you are too sad to pray, God's Spirit knows your heart and hears your prayer?

Another passage of Scripture that clearly indicates the Holy Spirit is God is Acts 5:3-4, the sad story of Ananias and Sapphira. They tried to deceive the apostles by stealing. Peter said, "Ananias, why has Satan filled your heart to lie to the Holy Spirit and keep back part of the proceeds from the field? Wasn't it yours while you possessed it? And after it was sold, wasn't it at your disposal? You have not lied to men but to God!"

Peter equates lying to the Holy Spirit with lying to God. By the way, you can't lie to a force. You can only lie to a person. The story of Ananias and Sapphira is a reminder that we should be honest with others; nothing escapes the oversight of God. Hebrews 4:13 says, "No creature is hidden from Him, but all things are naked and exposed to the eyes of Him to whom we must give an account."

# The Holy Spirit is a person

Notice that Jesus uses male personal pronouns when he speaks of sending to believers the Holy Spirit of promise. He never calls the Spirit an "it," but a "he." Jesus said, "He is the Spirit of truth. The world is unable to receive Him because it doesn't see Him or know Him. But you do know Him, because He remains with you and will be in you" (John 14:17).

When Jesus says he will send "another," he uses the Greek word *allos*, meaning "another of the same kind." Jesus could have easily used the Greek word *heteros*, which means "another of a different kind," but he did not. The Holy Spirit is of the same kind as God. He will *indwell* believers as Jesus had *dwelt with* believers in his public ministry.

These passages are amazing in that they promise the Holy Spirit will be with us forever and will abide in us. In Acts 2, we see that the Holy Spirit is poured out on the church. Believers are filled with God's Spirit, and three thousand people came into a relationship with Christ in one day (Acts 2:41).

Does God the Holy Spirit live in you? Have you realized you're a sinner in need of a Savior? Have you believed that your only hope in having a relationship with God is by trusting that Jesus took your just punishment by dying in your place on the cross? Have you believed that Christ not only died, but rose again on the third day? This raising of Jesus was proof that everything he said was true.

If you have believed, then the Holy Spirit lives in you. Make a practice of growing sensitive to his guidance in your life. Paul says in Galatians 5:16, "I say then, walk by the Spirit and you will not carry out the desire of the flesh." To walk by the Spirit is to obey God's Word and the counsel of the Spirit, who convicts you of sin. When you walk in the Spirit, you walk in step with the will of God.

# Questions to consider

1. Does the Holy Spirit try to attract people to himself or to someone else?

2. What are some differences between a force and a person?

3. How do we know the Holy Spirit is not a force?

4. Does Jesus call the Holy Spirit "it" or "he"?

# Truths to remember

1. The Holy Spirit always brings attention to Jesus. He draws our hearts to the sacrifice of Christ and to the truth of the gospel.

2. Many times in the Book of Acts, the Holy Spirit speaks. The Bible teaches that he is a person.

3. Jesus tells us that when he sends the Holy Spirit, he is sending us another of the same kind. The Holy Spirit is God.

4. When Ananias and Sapphira lied to the Holy Spirit, they didn't lie to men, but to God.

5. You can be filled with the Holy Spirit. When you become a believer, God takes up permanent residence in your life (John 14:23).

# Memory Verses

**WHO IS THE TRINITY?** "Listen, Israel: The LORD our God, the LORD is One" (Deut. 6:4).

**GOD IS ONE, GOD IS THREE:** "Go, therefore, and make disciples of all nations, baptizing them in the name of the Father and of the Son and of the Holy Spirit" (Matt. 28:19).

**GOD IS FATHER:** "There is one body and one Spirit — just as you were called to one hope at your calling — one Lord, one faith, one baptism, one God and Father of all, who is above all and through all and in all" (Eph. 4:4-6).

**GOD IS SON:** "In the beginning was the Word, and the Word was with God, and the Word was God. He was with God in the beginning. All things were created through Him, and apart from Him not one thing was created that has been created" (John 1:1-3).

**GOD IS HOLY SPIRIT:** "Now the Lord is the Spirit, and where the Spirit of the Lord is, there is freedom" (2 Cor. 3:17).

# PART 2 | What is Confession of Sin?

By Martin Winslow

We can all think of times when someone sinned against us. Maybe someone stole something from us or was unkind to us. We have all been wronged at one time or another. We have wronged others as well. We have been unfair, unloving, and unkind at different times. The reality that all of us have fallen short of doing what is right is called "sin." Sin separates us from God and others.

The word "sin" comes from a Greek word that means "missing the mark." Have you ever shot an arrow at a target and missed the bullseye? When we sin, it's like missing the target of God's perfect law. We're all guilty of sin. That's why Jesus came to perfectly fulfill God's law for us (Matt. 5:17).

Now that we know what sin is, what about the word "confession"? The Greek word for confession means "to agree or admit." The idea behind it is to declare oneself guilty of something. When we confess, we are agreeing or admitting that we made a mistake. As Christians, we're to confess our sins to God (1 John 1:9) and to others (Jas. 5:16). Confession of sin allows us to take responsibility for failure. It allows us to humble ourselves before God and others so that we can receive forgiveness.

Confession is a great, but difficult, thing to do. Humans have struggled with confession from the beginning. Our first parents, Adam and Eve, struggled with confessing their sins, and so do we. When Adam and Eve sinned, they immediately tried to hide themselves from the presence of God. Here is some of that story from Genesis 3:9-13:

So the LORD God called out to the man and said to him, "Where are you?"

And he said, "I heard You in the garden and I was afraid because I was naked, so I hid."

Then He asked, "Who told you that you were naked? Did you eat from the tree that I commanded you not to eat from?"

Then the man replied, "The woman You gave to be with me — she gave me some fruit from the tree, and I ate."

So the LORD God asked the woman, "What is this you have done?" And the woman said, "It was the serpent. He deceived me, and I ate."

Notice what happened when God confronted Adam and Eve. Adam blamed Eve, and Eve blamed the serpent. Neither of them confessed his or her sin, but instead tried to make excuses rather than take responsibility. Confession of sin helps a person take responsibility for an action that needs forgiveness.

I hope as you read this book and answer the questions, you begin to see the importance of confessing your sins to God and others. If you take responsibility for your failures, you're able to have strong relationships with others and, most importantly, with God. I recommend that parents read one chapter a night with their children and talk through the "Questions to consider" and "Truths to remember" at the end of the chapter.

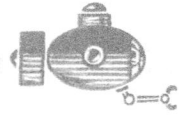

# PART 2.1 | Confession to God

### MEMORY VERSE - 1 JOHN 1:9
"If we confess our sins, He is faithful and righteous to forgive us our sins and to cleanse us from all unrighteousness."

## The greatest commandment

In the Gospel of Matthew, a lawyer came to Jesus and asked him to name the greatest commandment. Jesus answered him, "Love the Lord your God with all your heart, with all your soul, and with all your mind" (Matt. 22:37). This means we should love God with our whole being. We should make nothing a priority above serving God.

However, each of us falls short of this calling to love God with everything. Every one of us will sin against God by not putting him first at some point in our lives. Romans 3:10 says, "... as it is written, 'There is no one righteous, not even one.'" Each one of us is a sinner who needs to be saved. Because sin happens, confession must happen.

Have you made a habit of confessing your sins to God? It's important to realize your weaknesses and take responsibility for them. In the Sermon on the Mount, Jesus' expectation is for his disciples to be people of prayer. He doesn't say, "if you pray," but rather "when you pray," you should pray in a specific way.

In the Model Prayer, Jesus says we should pray, "And forgive us our debts, as we also have forgiven our debtors" (Matt. 6:12). The word "debts" here means "sins." Jesus says we should pray for forgiveness of our sins and forgive those who have sinned against us. Confessing these sins during prayer is one healthy way to humble ourselves before Almighty God.

# I thought I was already forgiven

You might be thinking, "Why should I confess my sins if I have already been forgiven through what Jesus accomplished for me on the cross?" This is a great question. It's true that when you believe the gospel and are born again, you receive forgiveness of your sins – past, present, and future.

Jesus' last words on the cross included *tetelestai*, "paid in full." Your sins were totally paid for on the cross, but as a way of continuing a healthy relationship with God, you and I must keep our hearts sensitive to sin. Confession is a way for us to acknowledge before God our weaknesses and our continued need for him.

If we don't confess and take responsibility for our sins, we can easily become hard-hearted toward sin. Hebrews 3:13 says, "But encourage each other daily, while it is still called today, so that none of you is hardened by sin's deception." Sin deceives us, and the longer we go without confessing, the more we allow our hearts to become hardened to sin.

In the Old Testament, we read the story of King Saul's life. Saul is a perfect example of what happens to someone who refuses to acknowledge sin in his or her life. After David killed Goliath, Saul became exceedingly jealous of David. Saul's sin of jealousy had taken such root in his life that, on many occasions, he tried to murder David without cause (1 Sam. 18:11, 13, 17, 20; 19:1, 10, 11, 18).

Saul knew he was sinning against David and even admitted it (1 Sam. 26:21), but he never turned to God in confession and repentance. Confession keeps the line of communication open between God and you.

In church life, we observe the Lord's Supper several times a year. The bread and juice serve to remind us of the body and blood of Jesus. When we eat the bread and drink the juice, we recognize the great sacrifice Jesus made on our behalf. Confession also reminds us of our need for a relationship with Jesus. It prompts us to get spiritually clean before God.

Once, when I was a youngster, we had a hard rain. The ditch across the street from my house had filled with water. My friends and I were running our bikes into this ditch for a couple of hours, having a blast. We were totally covered in mud. I remember that my mom wouldn't let me in the house until I had completely hosed off with water outside.

Being muddy didn't mean I wasn't my mother's son anymore. It did mean that while I was covered in mud, our relationship couldn't be quite the same. The mud had come between us. I wasn't free to run around in the house until the mud had been washed away. Confession works a lot like the water hose outside my house. When we sin, it doesn't mean we aren't children of God anymore. It does limit the relationship, though.

Our memory verse says, "If we confess our sins, He is faithful and righteous to forgive us our sins and to cleanse us from all unrighteousness" (1 John 1:9). Confess your sins to God and be cleansed again.

# Walls

When we sin, we naturally want to hide from God. Our sin becomes like a wall we build between us and God. When we enjoy our sins and are unwilling to admit they are a problem, we deceive ourselves. As 1 John 1:8 says, "If we say, 'We have no sin,' we are deceiving ourselves, and the truth is not in us." Notice that it says, "we are deceiving ourselves." It doesn't say we deceive God. God knows the truth, and it's impossible to hide from him.

The great historian Herodotus said that the walls of the ancient city of Babylon were eighty feet thick. Imagine how difficult it would be to break through a wall that thick. Over time, our continued sins in certain areas build up into thick walls because of our unwillingness to confess them. As this happens, it becomes more difficult to admit fault and take responsibility. Confession tears down these walls.

Confession allows you to live in a right relationship with God. Those walls of sin we place between us and God are barriers, but God sees right through them. The Scriptures teach us that nothing can be hidden from God. Hebrews 4:13 says, "No creature is hidden from Him, but all things are naked and exposed to the eyes of Him to whom we must give an account."

All things are open and laid bare before God. You and I cannot hide behind a wall from Almighty God. We might as well, as quickly as possible, confess whatever sins are hindering our relationship with him and remove those walls.

A great fourth-century Bible scholar and pastor named Augustine had a favorite verse: Proverbs 28:13. It says, "The one who conceals his sins will not prosper, but whoever confesses and renounces them will find mercy." To conceal a sin is to try to hide it. This verse says that whoever wants to find compassion from God must confess and turn away from sin.

## Questions to consider

1. Is it possible for us to love God with our whole being, or will we fail at this?

2. Does Jesus have anything to say to us about confessing our sins through prayer?

3. If Jesus has already forgiven us of all our sins, why should we confess sins we commit today?

4. What did King Saul try to do to David after refusing to confess and repent of the sin of jealousy?

## Truths to remember

1. For Christians, ongoing confession is healthy and cleanses us from sins we commit.

2. Unconfessed sin can lead to a hardened heart.

3. When we harden our hearts to God's truth and don't confess sin, we build walls between us and God.

4. No sin we commit is ever hidden from God. We should quickly take responsibility for our sins through confession.

# PART 2.2 | Confession to Others

MEMORY VERSE - JAS. 5:16
"Therefore, confess your sins to one another and pray for one another, so that you may be healed. The urgent request of a righteous person is very powerful in its effect."

## The cookies got me

Have you ever done something wrong and were so embarrassed that you hid it? Maybe someone asked if you had done something you shouldn't have, and you lied about it. Once, I snuck downstairs during Christmas time, got into the Santa Claus cookie jar when everyone was sleeping, and devoured a bunch of the chocolate chip cookies. Then, I carefully snuck back upstairs so that no one would hear me. I was feeling guilty but managed to get to sleep.

The next afternoon, when my father opened the cookie jar, he noticed most of the cookies were gone. He went around the room, asking who took them. Finally, he came to me. "Marty, did you eat these cookies?" I had the chance right then to confess my sin. I felt terrible inside. I knew what I had done was wrong, and I wanted to confess. Instead, I looked at my father and said, "It wasn't me."

He began to press me a little bit. "Are you sure you're telling the truth?" Here was my second chance to do the right thing. I looked him straight in the eyes and said, "No, it wasn't me." For a second time, I couldn't get myself to take responsibility. My insides were churning. I was almost physically sick because of my sin. I hated lying to my father, and knew in my heart that God knew what I had done. I needed to confess this sin.

Holding in a lie is a little bit like holding your breath. Try, right now, holding your breath for as long as you can. GO! Don't worry, I'll wait.

What happened at the end when you couldn't take it any longer? The same thing that happens to everyone. Your mouth bursts open, and you quickly suck in the oxygen your body needs. When you confess, you exhale all the carbon dioxide (sin) you had inside and quickly breathe in that fresh oxygen of forgiveness.

When I finally confessed the sin to my father, I felt free. It was like breathing in fresh air again. Do you need to confess sin to anyone?

# The second greatest commandment

Do you like it when someone lies to you? Would you like it if someone stole something from you? How about if someone called you a bad name or spread a rumor about you? Of course, you wouldn't want anyone to treat you this way. Instead, you would prefer truth, kindness, and consideration from others.

Jesus tells us that the second greatest commandment is to "love your neighbor as yourself" (Matt. 22:39). Do you think when Jesus says "neighbor," he's talking about your next-door neighbor? If so, you would be wrong. Your neighbor is any person with whom you come into contact. This can be your friend across the street, or at school, or maybe your brother or sister. Your neighbor is anyone.

The problem with the command to love your neighbor as yourself is not with the commandment. We are the problem. Many times, we fail to love others as much as we love ourselves. We sin against our neighbors by not being considerate of them. When we do this, we break the second greatest commandment. So, how do we go about making right the sins we have committed against others? We must confess our sins to them and ask forgiveness.

In the Gospel of Luke, Jesus tells the story of the prodigal son. The prodigal son treated his family, particularly his father, terribly by asking for his inheritance before his father was dead. Then, the prodigal went out and squandered his entire inheritance (the money his father had worked for his whole life) on riotous living.

After some hard times, the prodigal came to his senses and decided he was going to confess his sins to his father. In the story, the prodigal said, "I'll get up, go to my father, and say to him, 'Father, I have sinned against heaven and in your sight. I'm no longer worthy to be called your son. Make me like one of your hired hands'" (Luke 15:18-19).

Notice that the prodigal knew he had broken the first and second commandments. He had sinned against God and his father. In order to love his neighbor (his father) the way he would want to be loved, he had to confess his sin to his father. This confession of the prodigal broke the chains of sin on his life. His father was so excited to forgive and restore his son that he said, "... let's celebrate with a feast, because this son of mine was dead and is alive again; he was lost and is found!" (Luke 15:23-24).

If you have any unconfessed sin you have committed against someone, take some time, like the prodigal did, to think about what you need to say when you see that person again. When you do see him or her, confess your sin and ask forgiveness.

# Confess your sins first

When you sin against someone and know you made a mistake, you feel guilty. You might reason with yourself that if you just serve God better, it will make the mistake okay. Jesus said, instead of trying to serve God better or give an offering, it's more important to make things right with the other person first.

In the Sermon on the Mount, Jesus said:

> But if your eye is bad, your whole body will be full of darkness. So if the light within you is darkness — how deep is that darkness! No one can be a slave of two masters, since either he will hate one and love the other, or be devoted to one and despise the other. You cannot be slaves of God and of money (Matt. 6:23-24).

Notice that it's more important to Jesus that you make things right with your brother than it is to give an offering to the church.

Your brother here is not necessarily your sibling. You may have heard the expression, "They are my brothers and sisters in Christ." This passage refers to any Christian you may have offended with your sin. Go, confess to your brother or sister and make it right as quickly as you can.

When you confess your sin to your brother or sister, it's good for both of you. It helps the other person know that you value your relationship with him or her. It also teaches you to be humble, admit your faults, and receive forgiveness.

## Questions to consider

1. What is the second greatest commandment in the Bible?

2. What should I have quickly done when my father asked if I had eaten the Christmas cookies?

3. Is there anything you need to confess to your parents or to a friend?

4. Who is your neighbor? Is it your next-door neighbor? Who is your brother or sister? Is he or she necessarily your sibling?

## Truths to remember

1. Remember that when you are holding your breath, after a minute or so, you feel like you are going to explode. Holding in unconfessed sin can feel similar.

2. After holding your breath, when you take that next breath in, you feel great relief. Confessing your sin is like exhaling the carbon dioxide that builds up in your lungs. Taking in the oxygen is like taking in forgiveness. It is freeing and feels great.

3. The prodigal son confessed his sin to his father. When he did this, his relationship was restored. When we confess our sins to others, it breaks down walls we've built between us.

4. Jesus would rather you confess your sins to your brother first before giving an offering. To Jesus, your brother is more important than your money.

# PART 2.3 | The Power of Words

MEMORY VERSE - PS. 33:6
"The heavens were made by the word of the LORD, and all the stars, by the breath of His mouth."

## Words

I believe words are the most powerful things in the universe. Let me explain. Genesis 1:2-3 says,

> Now the earth was formless and empty, darkness covered the surface of the watery depths, and the Spirit of God was hovering over the surface of the waters. Then God *said*, "Let there be light," and there was light.

Notice that I emphasized the word "said." All God had to do was say the word, and the heavens and the earth were created. The power of his mighty word created the heavens and the earth instantly out of nothing. Talk about power!

In *The Magician's Nephew*, C. S. Lewis pictures the creation of the world called Narnia by the powerful voice of the lion, Aslan (a Christlike figure). By the singing voice of the lion, everything comes into existence out of nothing. At the end of his creative work, Aslan says, "Narnia, Narnia, Narnia, awake. Love. Think. Speak. Be walking trees. Be talking beasts. Be divine waters."[1] Lewis pictures something similar to what it must have been like during creation week.

Words are so powerful that the second person of the Trinity is called "the Word." Before God became man in the person of Jesus, God in three persons had always been. The second person of the Godhead is Jesus. Listen to John 1:1-3: "In the beginning was the Word, and the Word was with God, and the Word was God. He was with God in the beginning. All things were created through Him, and apart from Him not one thing was created that has been created."

Notice that these verses say the "Word was God" and created all things. John 1:14 says, "The Word became flesh and took up residence among us. We observed His glory, the glory as the One and Only Son from the Father, full of grace and truth." The Word that created everything and took on flesh (became a human) is Jesus. Can you imagine anyone more powerful than Jesus? And he is called "the Word."

# God's words and our words

Because God's words are so powerful, and we are made in his image, our words are very powerful as well. William Tyndale was a Bible scholar who believed all people should have the right to read the Word of God for themselves. Up until his time, the Bible was read in churches in Latin. Most people didn't understand Latin, so Tyndale wanted to translate a Bible into English for his people.

The King of England forbade Tyndale from making an English Bible translation, but Tyndale disobeyed him. He was arrested and tied to a stake. There, he was choked and burned to death. Why did the king want him dead? For translating God's Word.

Words cost Tyndale his life. Words are so powerful that we still know Tyndale's last words. Before he died at the stake, he said, "Lord, open the eyes of the King of England!"

God's words and our words are powerful things. People can lose their jobs for saying insensitive words. People are also honored and acclaimed for good words. Words have the power to hurt and the power to heal. Our words are more powerful than we are. In fact, someone may read the words on this page long after I'm dead. My words will outlast me. Because of this, we must make the most of our words.

# Sticks and stones

Have you ever heard the saying, "Sticks and stones may break my bones, but words will never hurt me"? Did you know this little saying is not true? Words can and do hurt. I can prove it.

Has anyone ever punched you in the arm or leg, or maybe even accidentally bumped into you and hurt you? It hurt because they physically harmed you, accidentally or not. Words can have harmful physical effects as well.

Has anyone ever said anything to you that made your stomach hurt? Have you ever gotten butterflies or started to sweat because of unkind words directed at you? Just like the pain of getting hit in the arm, unkind words can give you an unpleasant response in your body.

Words are sound waves – air vibrations – sent out from your mouth toward someone else. When the other person hears them, the air waves hit tiny hairs in the inner ear, and then the brain interprets the information as good or bad, positive or negative. Just like a blow from your hand, words from your mouth can "hit" in a physical way as well. That is why choosing words carefully is important.

# Say the right words

Now you see how important it is to use words when we confess our sins to God and others. Don't just say "I'm sorry" to your siblings when you've been unkind. Use the power of your words to specifically name your offense against them. Confess with words the specifics of the situation and then ask them to forgive you. Just saying you're sorry for something doesn't take full responsibility for the sin.

You and I need to own our sin. If your mother asked you to clean your room or take out the trash and you disobeyed her, how would you confess this sin? The right words might be something like this: "Mom, I know you asked me to take out the trash. I didn't obey you, and I sinned against you and God. Would you please forgive me for this?"

How about when you have spoken hatefully to a brother or sister? My brother's name is Mike. I might say, "Mike, I have no excuse for the way I talked to you. It was unkind and sinful. Would you please forgive me?" Taking complete responsibility like this demonstrates maturity and allows your words to express your heart.

Simply saying you're sorry doesn't acknowledge the sin. Detailed confession helps us name the sin aloud to God and others and receive the full power of forgiveness. Naming the sin is good for you and for the person you have sinned against. Just as words can "hit" the inner ear, causing pain, they also can enter gently and kindly with an uplifting effect. Confession is using the power of your words for the glory of God.

If you have some confessing to do to God or others, use your words to bring comfort and healing. Never say, "If you would stop doing this, I would stop sinning against you." That's rationalizing your sin. When you confess, forget what the other person did to you. Confession is for you to get your sin right with that person. Allow God's Spirit to move on his or her heart to get things right with you.

## Questions to consider

1. What does John 1:1 call Jesus?

2. What did God use to create?

3. Why did the King of England want to kill William Tyndale?

4. How can our words be like punching someone physically?

5. Why is saying "I'm sorry" not enough?

## Truths to remember

1. Jesus is called "the Word."

2. God created the universe by simply speaking the words.

3. Our words are very powerful things. They can bring others pain or comfort.

4. Confession of sin needs to be specific. Name the sin and ask for forgiveness. Own the sin.

5. The saying "sticks and stones" is not true. Words can and do hurt people.

# PART 2.4 | Confession and Pride

### MEMORY VERSE - JAS. 4:6
"But He gives greater grace. Therefore He says: God resists the proud, but gives grace to the humble."

## It's hard to be wrong

It's hard to be wrong. Has anyone ever pointed out to you a failure, and you immediately denied it, even though you knew it was valid? It's difficult for us to admit something we've done wrong because of pride. Being prideful means to look down upon others and exalt yourself above them.

The Book of Proverbs tells us that wisdom says, "Accept my instruction instead of silver, and knowledge rather than pure gold. For wisdom is better than jewels, and nothing desirable can compare with it" (Prov. 8:10-11). Wisdom and instruction should be more desirable to us than gold, silver, or even expensive jewels.

Pride has a way of keeping us from being completely honest about things. Prideful people hate hearing they made a mistake, so instead they make excuses for their wrong behavior. Pride and confession don't mix. Confession comes from a humble heart, never from a prideful heart.

Notice the memory verse above. "God resists the proud ...." That means God disapproves of the proud. That's a scary thought, isn't it? I don't want God opposed to or disapproving of me, do you?

If God is opposed to pride, then we ought to be opposed to it as well. We should be quick to listen to the Holy Spirit and to others about sins we've committed. We should be quick to confess the wrongs we've committed and not make excuses. Not admitting our wrongs is just our own pride, even when we know we're wrong.

Be okay with being wrong. We're all sinners who make mistakes and need to be forgiven. When you're wrong, don't make the situation worse by denying the wrong thing you did. Take responsibility and confess that sin to God and others. Quickly get your relationships corrected and on the right path. James 4:10 says, "Humble yourselves before the Lord, and He will exalt you."

# The broken CD player

My new truck was only one month old, and the CD player quit working. In the console of my truck, I always kept a little key that I needed to open my post office box. Mysteriously, the key disappeared at the same time. Two of my girls, ages two (Emma) and three (Anna), had been playing in my truck earlier in the day. I asked Anna if she had seen the key in my console. She said Emma had taken the key and shoved it in the CD player. Now my key was gone, and my new truck CD player was broken. I was upset but moved on.

Two years later, Emma and Anna were riding with me in the truck, and Anna said, "Dad, I have something to tell you." I said, "Yes, dear?" She said, "I was the one who put the key into your CD player, and I blamed it on Emma because she wasn't talking very well yet. Will you please forgive me?" I said, "Of course, I forgive you."

Isn't it crazy that even a child as young as three has trouble admitting she's done something wrong? Confession is difficult, no matter what your age. I asked Anna why she told me. She said that she felt bad all the time about doing it and had to tell me. When we have unconfessed sin, it's like a weight holding us down until we finally confess the sin and make it right.

In his classic book, *The Pilgrim's Progress,* John Bunyan talks about the moment the main character of the book, Christian, puts his trust in Christ to forgive his sin. Up until that point, Christian is carrying a huge burden of unconfessed sin on his back. When Christian gives his life to Jesus, this huge weight falls off his back and rolls down to the bottom of the hill.

Confession of sin feels like that huge weight being lifted, just as it did for my daughter, Anna, and the fictional character, Christian. Do you have sin you need to confess? Confess the sin and let the burden roll down to the bottom of the hill.

# Practice confession in your family

Confessing sin can be embarrassing. Because of the pride we struggle with, it's difficult to admit wrongdoing. A safe place to practice confession of sin is in your family. Proverbs 17:1 says, "Better a dry crust with peace than a house full of feasting with strife." This proverb says that it is better to nearly go hungry in a peaceful family than to be rich in a home full of fighting.

Do you agree with this proverb? Having harmony in your home with your parents and siblings is something for which you should strive every day of your life.

When there's strife in the home, it's like someone banging on random piano keys. The keys being hit in no particular order make a terrible noise. When there's love in the home, it's more like a beautiful piano piece played well. The notes being hit at precisely the right time make a pleasing sound and a calm atmosphere. When you sit down with your family to pray before bed, or at a morning devotional, stop and take time for confession of sin.

Confession can be done before the whole family or on an individual basis. Make sure to take full responsibility and say words that illustrate what you've done wrong. It may be difficult at first, but it's an incredibly important practice that helps us grow in our relationship with Christ and others.

My family regularly practices private and public confession of sin with each other. When I can tell there is some fussing going on among my children, I wait until the next devotional time, and we set time aside to confess to one another. Some of our confession times have been very powerful instruments for good in our family. There have been times when I was harsh with my children, and times that they were disrespectful to me. Our confession allows us to forgive one another.

If we want our Christianity to be more than just ideas, we must put into practice the things we know to be true. Confession of sin helps reconcile us with God and others. It also helps shape us into humble people who always realize our need for Jesus and relationships with others.

# The most important confession

I mentioned earlier that words are powerful. In fact, Romans 10:9-10 says, "If you confess with your mouth, 'Jesus is Lord,' and believe in your heart that God raised Him from the dead, you will be saved. One believes with the heart, resulting in righteousness, and one confesses with the mouth, resulting in salvation."

If you have not confessed your sins to Jesus and trusted that his death on the cross, in your place, purchased salvation for you, I invite you to do that. God desires a relationship with you. If you don't have a relationship with him, don't hold back. Confess your sins and let God forgive you. Trust Christ and believe the gospel.

# Questions to consider

1. Do you remember what two things should be more precious to us than gold, silver, and jewels?

2. God is opposed to the proud. What does this mean?

3. When the burden of sin fell off Christian's back in *The Pilgrim's Progress,* how do you think Christian felt?

4. If you said something harsh or mean to someone you know, practice out loud, right now, how you would confess that sin to the person. What would you say?

5. Are you a Christian? Have you made the most important confession, that Jesus is Lord of your life?

# Truths to remember

1. A family without harmony is like piano keys being banged randomly. It sounds terrible.

2. Confession of sin in a family setting is a safe place to get used to a life of confession of sin.

# Memory Verses

**CONFESSION TO GOD:** "If we confess our sins, He is faithful and righteous to forgive us our sins and to cleanse us from all unrighteousness" (1 John 1:9).

**CONFESSION TO OTHERS:** "Therefore, confess your sins to one another and pray for one another, so that you may be healed" (Jas. 5:16).

**THE POWER OF WORDS:** "The heavens were made by the word of the LORD, and all the stars, by the breath of His mouth" (Psalm 33:6).

**CONFESSION AND PRIDE:** "But He gives greater grace. Therefore He says: God resists the proud, but gives grace to the humble" (Jas. 4:6).

# PART 3 | What is Repentance?

By Martin Winslow

In 2004, I was in Houston, Texas, with a group from my church on a mission trip. One day, we were going from house to house, sharing about Jesus. As I approached one house, I realized I had made a mistake. I noticed out of the corner of my eye two huge dogs running toward me at top speed.

Seeing the danger, I turned and ran as fast as I could toward the street. The dogs chased me to the edge of the yard. When they came to the end of the grass at the sidewalk, they stopped in their tracks. They had either been trained not to cross the sidewalk, or they were wearing shock collars. To me, it didn't matter. I was glad to complete my escape.

The words "repent" and "repentance" occur seventy-three times in the New Testament. If God's Word speaks about it so many times, it must be important. "Repent" means "change your mind" or "turn around."

In my story above, as soon as I realized the error I had made in approaching the house, I changed my mind, turned around, and ran away from the trouble. If I had chosen to stay near the front door of that house, the dogs would have attacked me, and the story would have had a much different ending. Much like the dogs in the story, sin seeks to trap and attack us. Sin draws us in, and we forget that, like a dog, it will bite us.

Jesus tells us he came to call "sinners to repentance" (Luke 5:32). When we believe the gospel and trust in Jesus alone to save us, repentance becomes a way of life for Christians. When we realize that sin has lured us, and we have succumbed to temptation, we must repent – change our minds – about that sinful action and run back to the truth.

If you decide to stay in sin, it would be, like in the story above, letting the dogs attack you. When you change your mind about sin and return to the truth of God, it's like running to the safety of the street. We all sin at one time or another. Repentance is the commitment to run away from sin and back to God's truth when you realize your error.

Jesus' words in Mark 1:15 are, "The time is fulfilled, and the kingdom of God has come near. Repent and believe in the good news!"

Repentance can be very difficult for a Christian. It requires discipline, hard work, and prayer. It's important that we commit to a life of humble repentance. This allows our hearts to stay tender to the Word of God.

Thomas Watson was a Puritan who wrote a book called *The Doctrine of Repentance*.[1] He said there are six steps to repentance. I will use these steps as short chapters to help you better understand repentance. I recommend that parents read through one chapter a night with their kids and talk through the "Questions to consider" and "Truths to remember."

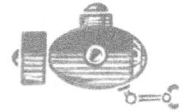

# PART 3.1 | Sight of Sin

MEMORY VERSE - HEB. 12:11
"No discipline seems enjoyable at the time, but painful. Later on, however, it yields the fruit of peace and righteousness to those who have been trained by it."

## See, then repent

Have you ever heard the saying, "Seeing is believing"? This is a proverb meaning, "You need to see something before you can accept that it is true." Sometimes, we must be shown our sin by others in order to accept that it's there. Do you clearly see your sins?

Have your parents ever told you to clean your room? When I was a kid, my mom would ask me to clean my room, and then, an hour later, she would ask me if I had finished. I would say yes. When she would come to inspect my room, I was always amazed at how many things she found undone. I didn't mean to do a bad job; I just didn't notice the details she would point out to me.

She would ask why there was a sock on the floor and why I hadn't vacuumed part of the carpet. She would point out that I didn't get all the dust off my dresser. Honestly, it was sometimes a little depressing for her to point it out. I hadn't noticed all the spots that were unclean in my room until she identified them. In order for me to fix the problems in my room, I had to see them.

Sin is sometimes like that sock on the floor, or dust on your dresser that you don't notice. It doesn't belong there, and it needs to be addressed, but if it's not pointed out, it just remains unfinished business. Before we can repent of sin, we must first see it. God has given us authorities in our lives that help point out those difficult-to-spot sins.

# God uses parents to help us see our sin

Your parents love you deeply. They want to watch you grow up to become a strong Christian. One way they help guide you toward a relationship with Jesus is by pointing out sin in your life. When they do point out sin in your life, do you listen and take responsibility? Or, do you defend yourself and make excuses? It's important to take responsibility for your sin. If you don't, you can never change your mind about it and repent.

Parents not only cheer you on and praise the great things you do; they also help you see your faults and failures. This is a good thing. The reason they show you your sin is so you can ask forgiveness and have your relationship with God and others restored.

When your parents point out your sin, it may be hard to hear at first. The Bible tells us that being disciplined for sin is tough. Hebrews 12:11 says, "No discipline seems enjoyable at the time, but painful. Later on, however, it yields the fruit of peace and righteousness to those who have been trained by it." Parents point out sin so that you might be trained to spot the differences between truth and lies.

You can help your parents by inviting them to point out things they see in your life that may not please God. Ask them to point out sin so that you may see it and ask God to help you change your mind and repent of it.

# God uses the church to help us see our sin

If you've attended church for very long, you've probably heard of King David. He was Israel's most famous king, other than Jesus. David was the warrior who defeated Goliath, unified Israel, and conquered many of his enemies. David was also a musician and a poet. He was a gifted person.

Once, when his men were out to war, he fell into sin by stealing Bathsheba, a beautiful young woman, from her husband, Uriah. David later had Uriah killed so he could cover his sin. Just when David thought he had gotten away with it, a prophet named Nathan told David a parable.

This parable allowed David to see his sin for what it was. David realized the seriousness of his sin and wrote a psalm to God that says, "Against You — You alone — I have sinned" (Ps. 51:4). David's heart had grown hard to his sin, but God used Nathan to show him his error.

In the New Testament, Jesus also tells us that if we notice sin in another Christian's life, we should help that person see it (Matt. 18:15-20). We should go to that person privately and kindly point out the sin he or she is committing.

If that person listens to you, Jesus says, "you have won them over." But if he or she doesn't listen, then you're to take others with you to again show the mistake to the Christian. If he or she still refuses to repent, then that sin is to be brought before the church. Hopefully, if someone shows you or me our sin, we're quick to see it and repent of it.

# God uses his Holy Spirit to help us see our sin

If you're a Christian, you have received the gift of the Holy Spirit. The Holy Spirit is the third person of the triune God we serve. We believe in God the Father, God the Son, and God the Holy Spirit, yet there is only one God.

God the Holy Spirit lives inside Christians. As 1 Corinthians 3:16 says, "Don't you yourselves know that you are God's sanctuary and that the Spirit of God lives in you?" Jesus said that when the Holy Spirit comes to live inside Christians, "He will convict the world about sin, righteousness, and judgment ..."(John 16:8). This means God's Spirit will remind you of what God expects from you, and you will see where you fall short.

If your parents ask you whether all your homework is finished, and you say it is, but you know you're really planning to finish it at school in the morning, you are lying to them. The Holy Spirit may be telling you in your heart that this is wrong. Will you listen to him and walk in God's Spirit, or ignore the truth and walk in the flesh?

The Bible says to not "harden your heart" against God's Spirit (Heb. 3:15). God wants to mold you into the person he desires you to be. Jesus says that a blind man cannot lead another blind man. If he does, both of them "will fall into a pit" (Luke 6:39). One of the two persons must be able to see clearly so that they don't both get injured. The Holy Spirit guides you into all the truth (John 16:13).

John Newton, a famous songwriter who used to buy and sell slaves before becoming a Christian and repenting of this horrible sin, wrote a famous song called "Amazing Grace." One of the lines in the song says, "I once was lost, but now I'm found, was blind but now I see." Let God use family, the church, and his Spirit to open your eyes to sin, so you might see clearly and turn from your sin. To repent of sin, you must first have "sight of sin."

# Questions to consider

1. Do you invite your parents to point out your sins so that you might grow to be more like Jesus?

2. Do you have Christian friends in the church who are willing to tell you when you are in sin?

3. Do you listen to the Holy Spirit in your life when he warns you about your sin?

4. Do you want to see your sin, or ignore it?

# Truths to remember

1. You will never be perfect in this life. Jesus was perfect in your place.

2. Jesus paid for all our sins on the cross. Repentance is our way of remembering his great sacrifice in our place and turning from our sins out of love for Jesus.

# PART 3.2 | Sorrow for Sin

MEMORY VERSE - PS. 51:3
"For I am conscious of my rebellion, and my sin is always before me."

## Sorrow must be sincere

Have your parents ever caught you fighting with a sibling and told you to say you were sorry? Did you quickly say the word "sorry," but you didn't really mean it? At one time or another, we have all said we're sorry but didn't mean it. Sometimes, we need time to think about what we have done before we can truly feel sorrow for our bad behavior. The emotions and anger we feel in the moment can keep our "sorry" from being genuine.

When I was in third grade, I got into a fight with my best friend, Brad. We started punching and kicking each other. Our parents heard us fighting and brought us together and told us to shake hands and say we were sorry. Brad put out his hand to shake mine and said he was sorry. My parents kept telling me to do the same, but there was no way I was going to do it. At that moment, I wasn't sorry; I was still mad.

If I had reached out my hand to shake Brad's in that moment, would it have been sincere? No, I needed time to think about what happened. I needed time to realize that my relationship with my best friend was now broken. I needed time to realize that my sin was against God, because I was trying to hurt Brad, and Brad was made in God's image.

Being sorry isn't the same as saying you're sorry. Sorrow is a deep feeling of grief that overcomes you for a sin or sins you have committed. After King David's sin with Bathsheba, he said, "my sin is always before me" (Ps. 51:3). This means he was feeling sadness and grief from his sin. Sorrow from the sin felt to David like it was always in front of his face. He couldn't get away from the sorrow his sin had caused. David was feeling true sorrow and wanted his sin to be forgiven.

Have you ever felt this way? After fighting with a sibling, telling a lie, cheating on a test, or speaking unkindly to someone, it's normal to have a feeling of sorrow in your heart. As a Christian, it's important what you do with that sorrow.

# Don't ignore sorrow

Sometimes, instead of allowing a sorrow to drive you toward forgiveness and making things right with others, you allow it to bottle up inside you. The Holy Spirit may be convicting you of your sin, and instead of making things right, you avoid dealing with the issue. The Bible says in 1 Thessalonians 5:19, "Don't stifle the Spirit."

If you threw a wet blanket on a tiny fire, the blanket would put out the flames. When you ignore sorrow that's in your life from sin, it's like putting a wet blanket over God's Holy Spirit. Instead of ignoring God's Spirit, we need to respond to his work in our hearts.

If we don't respond to the Holy Spirit, our hearts can grow hard. Proverbs 28:13-14 says, "The one who conceals his sins will not prosper, but whoever confesses and renounces them will find mercy. Happy is the one who is always reverent, but one who hardens his heart falls into trouble."

If we harden our hearts against God, we fall into trouble, or calamity. Instead, we must confess our mistakes, deal with our sorrow, and turn toward God. God is always quick to forgive us. In 1 John 1:9, we learn, "If we confess our sins, He is faithful and righteous to forgive us our sins and to cleanse us from all unrighteousness."

If you ignore the sorrow that comes from sin, you will not find forgiveness and freedom. If you respond to the sorrow rather than hardening your heart, it will lead to forgiveness and freedom.

# Sorry you got caught, or truly sorry?

There's an important difference between being sorry you got caught doing something wrong and truly being sorry. Let me explain.

A few years ago, when I was a principal at a Christian school, an interesting thing happened. It was early Monday morning, and I was setting up the chapel for the students who would be arriving soon. A little girl had come in earlier than the other students and looked very sad. I didn't say anything to her, but just kept setting up the chairs in the chapel.

Then she walked up to me. I asked her if she needed something, and she suddenly burst into tears. She said, "Mr. Winslow, can you ever forgive me?" I told her to come to my office to talk. After she sat down, she said that the previous Friday afternoon, she had cheated on a Latin test. She said that all weekend she kept thinking about the sin she had committed, and she needed to confess that sin and was truly sorry for what she had done.

This student didn't get caught cheating; she confessed to cheating. The Holy Spirit had convicted her of her sin, and she couldn't move on until she dealt with the sorrow inside her by confessing the sin to me. She was a perfect example of what David said, "my sin is always before me." The student was truly sorry.

Being sorry you got caught is different. Let's say this same student had been caught cheating on the test and was sent to the principal's office. She may still be sad and cry, but only because she got caught, rather than because sin offends God and separates us from God and others. It may take being caught for you to be truly sorry, but it's always best if the sorrow comes from God convicting your heart about your sin, and not just because you were caught.

# Godly sorrow

The Bible speaks of a "godly sorrow" and a "worldly sorrow." Paul says in 2 Corinthians 7:10, "For godly grief produces a repentance not to be regretted and leading to salvation, but worldly grief produces death."

The story I told of the student above is a perfect example of godly sorrow. The conviction that came upon her heart from the sin of cheating left her desiring forgiveness. She wanted to turn from the sin of cheating and get right with me (the principal) and God. When she had done this, she felt great relief and thankfulness for the forgiveness extended to her.

Notice that Paul also says there is a worldly sorrow that produces death. This is the type of sorrow that only comes the moment people are caught doing something they shouldn't. Conviction only comes when someone else points out the wrong they have done. There is no real desire in sinners to change and be more like Jesus. They simply don't want to be caught having done something wrong.

A perfect example of this in the New Testament is Judas Iscariot. Judas was given thirty pieces of silver to betray Jesus. After he betrayed Jesus, he came back and said he had betrayed "innocent blood" (Matt. 27:4). He even threw back the money to the chief priests. His sorrow was not a godly sorrow that leads to repentance. His sorrow was because he had been recognized by Jesus, all the disciples, and everyone else present at Jesus' arrest, as the one who betrayed Jesus.

Judas was simply caught. He may have thrown the money back, but instead of repentance that leads to forgiveness and salvation, his worldly sorrow never moved him to ask God for forgiveness (Matt. 27:5). Pray that God would give you "sight of sin" and true "sorrow over your sin," so you can sincerely repent.

## Questions to consider

1. Are you sorry when you get caught sinning, or sorry for the sin itself?

2. Is your sin like David's, always before you? Do you quickly forget your sins?

3. Is there anyone you need to tell you are sorry? What is keeping you from doing it?

## Truths to remember

1. Sometimes you may need time to feel genuinely sorry for sin. Reflect on this.

2. Sorrow is deep grief and sadness over your sin that moves you toward repentance.

# PART 3.3 | Confession of Sin

MEMORY VERSE - 1 JOHN 1:9
"If we confess our sins, He is faithful and righteous to forgive us our sins and to cleanse us from all unrighteousness."

## Taking responsibility for our sin

I felt like a huge weight had been lifted off my chest! It was a moment I will never forget. I was seventeen years old, and I was feeling the grief and pain of my sin. I could see my sins were many, and I was truly sorrowful for them.

I went to the youth minister of my church and confessed my sins to him and to God and asked for forgiveness. I asked Jesus to forgive me for offending him by my evil way of life. I trusted in that moment that he had died for my sins and risen again for me.

In that moment, I was "born again." This was the day I became a Christian, but my repenting of sin was just beginning.

Paul talks about two ways that characterize Christian living. One way is called "walking in the Spirit," and the other is called "walking in the flesh." Paul also says, "For the flesh desires what is against the Spirit, and the Spirit desires what is against the flesh; these are opposed to each other, so that you don't do what you want" (Gal. 5:17). What Paul is saying here is that even though you might be a Christian, sometimes you will not walk by God's Spirit.

When we choose to do things that are displeasing to God, you and I are "walking in the flesh." Since we are all children of Adam and Eve, we inherited bodies that are susceptible to sin. When we give in to the sins of the world, we are "walking in the flesh."

If you're a Christian, you have also received the gift of the Holy Spirit. Paul says, "Don't you know that your body is a sanctuary of the Holy Spirit who is in you, whom you have from God? You are not your own, for you were bought at a price. Therefore glorify God in your body" (1 Cor. 6:19-20).

When we choose to obey God and his commands, we are "walking in the Spirit." If you are a Christian, you notice that it doesn't mean you live a perfect life. Sometimes, you walk in the flesh and break God's commands. This is why we must confess our sins and turn from them.

When we do walk in the flesh, we should be quick to confess these things to God, and to others we may have offended. If we wish to grow into strong Christians, we must be willing to take responsibility for our shortcomings and confess them to others. Part of growing as a Christian is taking responsibility quickly for sin.

# Confessing to God

When I became a Christian, it involved taking responsibility for my sins and confessing them to Jesus. While becoming a Christian is a one-time event (you can't be born again more than once), confession is not a one-time event. Even though you were forgiven of your sins of the past, present, and future, it's still a good practice for your ongoing relationship with him to confess your sins to God.

When Jesus taught his disciples to pray, he said in the Model Prayer, "And forgive us our debts, as we also have forgiven our debtors" (Matt. 6:12).

If I have a relationship with God, and I know that I have sinned against him, it's right for me to confess my sin and ask for forgiveness. This confession isn't out of fear that I am not a Christian anymore, or that God has turned his back on me. This confession is because I love Jesus. I want to live my life for him. I want to be used by him as an example of what a changed life looks like.

When I confess my sins to him, I am recognizing my inability to live a godly life without his help. I am admitting my weaknesses to him and asking him to forgive me and live through me even more. How can I ever repent and turn to God if I don't confess my sins to him?

I quoted this verse earlier but will do it again here: "The one who conceals his sins will not prosper, but whoever confesses and renounces them will find mercy" (Prov. 28:13). Both confession of sin and forsaking of sin are mentioned here. To forsake the sin is to repent or stop practicing the sin. Galatians 5:16 says, "… walk by the Spirit and you will not carry out the desire of the flesh."

# Confessing to others

Words do hurt others. Words are powerful. We can use them to build up and encourage, or we can use them to tear down and destroy. I am sure someone has said something at some time that hurt your feelings. When that happened, do you remember that your stomach hurt, or you wanted to cry, or it made you feel down? Words are powerful and can be used for good or evil.

When we confess our sins to people we have hurt, it can help heal them and our relationship with them. If the confession is forced upon you by someone else, and you really don't want to take responsibility, the person you are confessing to will know you don't mean it. However, if you've had a change of heart, and God has opened your eyes to see your sin, and you are sorrowful for it, then confession of that sin can be an encouraging thing to the offended person.

One time, I said some things to someone in an uncaring way. I had reasoned with myself that what I said was the truth. It wasn't so much the truth of what I said; it was the way I said it. The way I said it hurt someone's feelings. At the moment, I wasn't sensitive to that person's feelings. All I cared about was the truth. What I failed to realize was that there is a way to be both truthful and loving at the same time.

The second greatest commandment in the Bible is to love your neighbor as yourself. In that moment, I was loving truth more than my neighbor. This sin of mine had caused damage to the relationship. I prayed about this situation, and God revealed to me that I should ask forgiveness. I went to that person one evening and spelled out what I had done and why it was wrong. I told them that I understood why they felt that way toward me and that I had been the one to create the barrier between us. Then I asked for forgiveness.

First, I gave a detailed confession. I named what I had done wrong. This was probably the hardest part, because in that moment I had to humble myself enough to take total responsibility for the mess I had created. Confessing your sin is owning every bit of it.

# Ongoing confession for the Christian

Make a practice of not just saying the word "sorry" to someone else. Tell that person what you've done. Take responsibility, and ask him or her for specific forgiveness for the sin you've committed. See the sin, be sorrowful, and confess your sins to God and others. Is there anything right now that you need to confess? If so, what are you waiting for?

# Questions to consider

1. Do you remember what it means to walk in the Spirit? What about walking in the flesh?

2. Are there any sins you need to confess to God? What about to others you have hurt?

3. Are you able to humble yourself enough to confess your sins to those you have hurt?

# Truths to remember

1. You have two choices today as a Christian. You can walk in the Spirit or you can walk in the flesh.

2. Becoming a Christian is a one-time event, but confession should be ongoing for the Christian.

3. Be detailed if you are going to confess something you did that hurt someone. Own it.

# PART 3.4 | Shame of Sin

**MEMORY VERSE - HEB. 12:2**
"… keeping our eyes on Jesus, the source and perfecter of our faith, who for the joy that lay before Him endured a cross and despised the shame and has sat down at the right hand of God's throne."

John Piper says there are two types of shame in the Bible. One he calls a "misplaced shame (the kind we ought not to have)," and the other "well-placed shame (the kind we ought to have)."

Misplaced shame is misplaced because there is no reason to have it. Paul says, "For I am not ashamed of the gospel, because it is God's power for salvation to everyone who believes, first to the Jew, and also to the Greek" (Rom. 1:16). This would be shame that we shouldn't have. The gospel is true, and it saves men and women. To be ashamed of it is misplaced shame.

Jesus said, "For whoever is ashamed of Me and My words, the Son of Man will be ashamed of him when He comes in His glory and that of the Father and the holy angels" (Luke 9:26). If you are ashamed of the words of Jesus, this again is a misplaced shame. It doesn't matter if the world mocks you or makes fun of you; you should never be ashamed of Christ's words. There is no reason for you to be ashamed of what Jesus has said.

Well-placed shame is the shame a Christian feels for committing sin against a holy God. As Piper says, "Sin is always a proper cause for shame because sin is behavior that dishonors God."[2]

Shame is a powerful emotion, not unlike sorrow. When shame comes from a sinful act that needs to be confessed, it can be used to draw us closer to God. The shame we feel from sin needs to be channeled in the right direction. Jesus gives us guidance on how to deal with the shame of sin in our lives.

In Luke's Gospel, there's a powerful story of a woman who had committed some serious sins. She came to Jesus seeking forgiveness.

Luke tells us:

> Then one of the Pharisees invited Him to eat with him. He entered the Pharisee's house and reclined at the table. And a woman in the town who was a sinner found out that Jesus was reclining at the table in the Pharisee's house. She brought an alabaster jar of fragrant oil and stood behind Him at His feet, weeping, and began to wash His feet with her tears. She wiped His feet with the hair of her head, kissing them and anointing them with the fragrant oil. When the Pharisee who had invited Him saw this, he said to himself, "This man, if He were a prophet, would know who and what kind of woman this is who is touching Him — she's a sinner!" (Luke 7:36-39).

The woman in this story was deeply distressed by her sin. We read that she was weeping enough so that Jesus' feet could be washed with her tears. Imagine how many tears that would take. She was feeling the shame of her sin and her need of forgiveness. The Pharisee in the story thought Jesus shouldn't have allowed the woman to perform this act of humility. If the Pharisee had his way, the woman would have remained in her sin and shame.

But Jesus doesn't treat us like that. Instead, he says to the Pharisee:

> "Therefore I tell you, her many sins have been forgiven; that's why she loved much. But the one who is forgiven little, loves little." Then Jesus said to her, "Your sins are forgiven." Those at the table with Jesus began to say among themselves, "Who is this man who even forgives sins?" Jesus said to the woman, "Your faith has saved you. Go in peace" (Luke 7:47-50).

You notice in the story that Jesus says to her, "Your faith has saved you. Go in peace." Shame over sin is healthy to draw us to the life-giving power of Christ's forgiveness. But you must not forget that Jesus tells all his children to see their sin, grieve their sin, and confess their sin. Because Jesus bore the reproach of sin for our sakes, he tells us, "Go in peace."

# No longer ashamed

For a Christian to be ashamed of a sinful act is healthy, but to stay ashamed after that sin has been forgiven is to deny the power of Christ's forgiveness. Hebrews 12:2 says, "... keeping our eyes on Jesus, the source and perfecter of our faith, who for the joy that lay before Him endured a cross and despised the shame and has sat down at the right hand of God's throne."

This passage tells us that Jesus "despised" the shame of the cross. This means Jesus was willing to take the shame of all our sins and die for them on the cross. The curse of the cross, and its pain and suffering, were realities Jesus willingly took upon himself. Our shame from sin was placed upon Jesus.

In the Garden of Eden, when Eve was first given to Adam, the Bible says they "were naked and not ashamed." When sin entered the world, the first thing Adam and Eve did was sew fig leaves together to cover themselves. When they became sinful, they were immediately ashamed.

Do you remember what God did next for Adam and Eve in the story? "The LORD God made clothing out of skins for Adam and his wife, and He clothed them" (Gen. 3:21). An animal died, and God covered Adam and Eve with the skin of the animal. When the animal died, its life was taken in place of theirs. Its blood was shed to save them, and its body was given to cover them.

The same thing happened in the New Testament with Jesus, but in a perfect way. Instead of an animal dying in our place, the perfect Son of God died in our place. He took all our sin and shame upon himself. Hebrews 1:3 says that after he had done this, "He sat down at the right hand of the Majesty on high." A person only sits down when the work has been done. Jesus died for all your shame and guilt.

# Put your shame on the cross

Shame is a natural feeling you have as a Christian when you sin against God. That feeling is meant to drive you to repentance. It's not healthy to stay in shame. Remember that Christ died for all your sin and shame. You must not only accept forgiveness from Christ; you must also forgive yourself.

Living in guilt denies the power of what Jesus accomplished for you on the cross. Among Jesus' last words on the cross were, "It is finished!" (John 19:30). Let shame drive you to Jesus, but then accept the same words he spoke to the woman who washed his feet: "Go in peace."

## Questions to consider

1. Have you been ashamed of your sins?

2. Do you stay ashamed of your sins, or have you trusted Jesus to forgive you?

3. Do you have any well-placed shame that you haven't confessed to God?

## Truths to remember

1. There's a difference between misplaced shame and well-placed shame.

2. The sinful woman's tears showed how ashamed she was of her sin.

3. Jesus told her, "Go in peace." Her shame led her to the feet of Christ, and she was forgiven.

4. When you place the guilt and shame of your sins at the feet of Jesus, he will say, "Go in peace."

# PART 3.5 | Hatred of Sin

MEMORY VERSE - ROM. 6:23
"For the wages of sin is death, but the gift of God is
eternal life in Christ Jesus our Lord."

## Hate sin, not people

Is it okay to hate? Your parents probably told you that it's not okay to hate someone. I totally agree with them. It's not okay. In fact, it's the opposite of what God calls Christians to do. Jesus said, "Love the Lord your God with all your heart, with all your soul, with all your mind, and with all your strength" (Mark 12:30). In the next verse, he said that the second greatest commandment is to "love your neighbor as yourself."

Jesus even said in the Sermon on the Mount, "But I tell you, love your enemies and pray for those who persecute you" (Matt. 5:44). Jesus told his disciples the whole world would know his disciples by the love they have for one another (John 13:35).

Loving others is critical for a Christian. Jesus said, "No greater love has any man than this, that He lay down His life for His friends" (John 15:13). John 3:16 says, "For God loved the world in this way: He gave His One and Only Son, so that everyone who believes in Him will not perish but have eternal life."

As you can see from looking at Jesus' words, it's not okay to hate people. In fact, we must love all people, even enemies. But it is okay to hate sin. Our sin builds "barriers between you and your God" (Isa. 59:2), "ensnares us" (Heb. 12:1), "enslaves us" (John 8:34), and ultimately earns us death (Rom. 6:23).

# Sin separates us from God and others

When Adam and Eve sinned, they hid from God. What do you and I naturally want to do when we sin? We hide it. When we hide sin, we cannot have good relationships with God and others. In order to restore those relationships, we must quickly take responsibility for sin, confess it, and turn from it.

Fortunately, Scripture tells us, "The LORD is gracious and compassionate, slow to anger and great in faithful love" (Ps. 145:8). God, through the sacrifice of Christ, takes away the separation that existed between him and us.

When we believe in what he's done for us, we're able to have a relationship with him. He also tells us that we must extend forgiveness to others. We must forgive as we have been forgiven. Jesus said, "For if you forgive people their wrongdoing, your heavenly Father will forgive you as well. But if you don't forgive people, your Father will not forgive your wrongdoing" (Matt. 6:14-15).

How many times should we forgive someone who has sinned against us? Peter asked this important question, and Jesus told him, "up to seventy times seven" (Matt. 18:22). Wow! Jesus' point is that we should never stop forgiving others.

But what is it that causes us to need forgiveness in the first place? It's sin. God made us to have a relationship with him and others. Sin creates barriers between God and us, and between others and us. Because of this, we must hate sin. If we decide to love our sin instead, we will never repent or turn from it. Why would we want to turn from something we actually love?

The Bible tells us that God is holy and separate from sin and evil (Isa. 6:3). We are also called, in 1 Peter 1:16, to "Be holy, because I am holy." The only way for us to strive toward rooting sin out of our lives is to hate sin.

# Sin is the cause of all the problems in the world

Sin didn't just affect you and me. Sin affected and infected the whole world. Genesis 3:14-19 shows us the whole world was affected by the sin of Adam and Eve. Animals were cursed, people were banished, and the ground was cursed.

Romans 8:22-23 says, "For we know that the whole creation has been groaning together with labor pains until now. And not only that, but we ourselves who have the Spirit as the firstfruits — we also groan within ourselves, eagerly waiting for adoption, the redemption of our bodies." This means the entire creation is waiting to be born again. Revelation 21 tells us there will be new heavens and a new earth. The old earth that was cursed will pass away (see also 2 Pet. 3).

We also continue to struggle with sin in our lives as Christians. Even though we have been forgiven and spiritually reborn, the flesh in which we still live is weak and reminds us that it must be made new again when Christ returns (1 Thess. 4; 1 Cor. 15). Jesus came into this world to reverse the curse of sin. He defeated sin and killed it on the cross. In 1 John 3:8, the apostle says, "The Son of God was revealed for this purpose: to destroy the Devil's works."

Christians must agree with God that sin is evil, and therefore hate it. This hatred of sin in the power of God's Spirit allows us to have victory in turning from sin even today. Remember that your repentance will never be perfect in this life.

John writes, "My little children, I am writing you these things so that you may not sin. But if anyone does sin, we have an advocate with the Father — Jesus Christ the Righteous One" (1 John 2:1). John is saying that we should do our best to live lives without sin. But, since sometimes we still mess up, remember that Christ is our advocate. He continues to forgive us, even now.

# Jesus got angry at death and so should we!

Look at our memory verse above. Do you see what causes death? Sin causes death. God made us for life. He wants us to have abundant life, but sin tries to tear us down and destroy us spiritually and physically.

There's a story in the New Testament you probably know. It's the story of Lazarus. Many people remember that the shortest verse in the Bible comes from this story in John 11. Do you know that the shortest verse says, "Jesus wept"? He was weeping in the story because his friend, Lazarus, had died.

Lazarus was a sinner, just like the rest of us, and had become ill. This sickness ultimately led to his death. Now, Jesus had come to Bethany where

Lazarus lived, and he saw the emotion and pain of those mourning the death of his friend. Jesus was overcome with emotion, and he too cried at the situation.

There's an interesting Greek word used in this story. It is used in both John 11:33 and 11:38. Many Bible versions say it means Jesus was "deeply moved." However, the word is used in classical Greek to describe horses snorting as they prepare for battle. In the Septuagint, the Greek version of the Old Testament, the word can mean "indignation" (Lam. 2:6) and "rage" (Dan. 11:30). Instead of translating the word "deeply moved" by Lazarus' death, many believe a better translation would be that Jesus was angry.

J. Scott Duvall, in his book, *Devotions on the Greek New Testament,* says:

> As Jesus goes to the tomb of Lazarus, he isn't just overwhelmed with sadness and grief. He's also righteous with rage. He's fighting mad. He's angry at sin, suffering, disease and most of all death! He's furious at these evil powers for hurting the people he loves so deeply.[3]

Do you remember what Jesus does in the story of Lazarus? He demonstrates his power over both sin and death by calling Lazarus forth from the tomb. He defeats both sin and death through his power. Jesus hates sin! He also hates the death that comes from it. If we are going to repent and turn from our sins, we must pray that God helps us hate our sin.

# Questions to consider

1. Do you love your sin or hate it?

2. Is it okay to hate sin? Does that mean we hate people, since people sin?

3. What emotion did Jesus feel when he saw that his friend, Lazarus, had died?

# Truths to remember

1. Sin earns us death. We need Jesus because he conquered both sin and death for us.

2. God is holy, and he calls each of his followers to be holy as well.

3. You will never turn from sin if you love it.

4. Sin is the cause of all the problems in the world, not just our personal problems.

# PART 3.6 | Turning from Sin

## MEMORY VERSE - MATT. 3:8
"Therefore produce fruit consistent with repentance."

# Christians repent of their sins

How do you know that an apple tree is an apple tree? Does it not have apples on it? You know a lemon tree is a lemon tree because it has lemons on it. A tree is known by its fruit. Christians are people who repent of their sins. When we are confronted by God's Word, the Holy Spirit, or others, our natural desire should be to put that sin to death and turn from it. This means when we repent, we are producing the kind of fruit that would identify us as Christians.

In the memory verse above, John the Baptist is telling the religious leaders their repentance should be evident in the way they live their lives. After you've seen sin, been sorrowful over it, confessed it, felt shame for it, and hated it, you are ready to turn from it. It will be hard work. You will be tempted to sin every day of your life. This is normal because sin has infected us, and we are in a battle to live holy lives.

When you fall short, remember that you are saved by God's grace. That means you cannot earn his favor by being good. You must rest in the fact that he gave you the gift of salvation. Don't forget that he has also called you to repent of your sins.

To the best of our ability, with the help of the Holy Spirit, we should turn from sin and strive for godly living. Living in God's will gives us joy and peace. Strive for this in your life with God and others. Live at peace with your brothers, sisters, friends, and family. Live at peace with God.

# Easy to understand, hard to do

I remember watching major league baseball on TV as a kid. Watching the screen, it didn't look that hard to hit a fastball from a professional pitcher. Then as I grew up, I remember the first time I saw a pitch sail by me at 90 m.p.h. I realized then that hitting the ball was easier said than done.

Overcoming sin in your life is the same way. It's easy to talk about, but very difficult to put into practice. Sometimes we like the sin we're committing. Sometimes we don't even think about the sin, we just do it. Sometimes we sin because we care about what someone else thinks about us and we want to fit in. Sometimes we just get angry, or don't want to obey authority. There are a million reasons why we fail, but keeping a soft heart toward the Word of God is very important to overcoming sin.

When you believed the gospel and became a Christian, you began a difficult journey. There was no magic wand waved over you that ended all your difficulties when you became a Christian. In fact, Jesus said in Luke 9 that if you want to follow him, you must pick up your cross daily and follow him. In Matthew 7:14, he says, "Narrow is the gate and difficult the road that leads to life."

It's difficult being a Christian. It's a commitment. Paul compares his Christian journey to athletic games: "Therefore I do not run like one who runs aimlessly or box like one beating the air. Instead, I discipline my body and bring it under strict control, so that after preaching to others, I myself will not be disqualified" (1 Cor. 9:26-27).

Paul had disciplined himself to overcome sin to the best of his ability. If his body or mind wanted to do something he knew was against a command of God, he disciplined his body to make it his "slave."

Famous athletes today sometimes spend over a million dollars per year to keep their bodies in shape for the sport to which they have dedicated themselves. Every piece of food, every training session, every hour in the gym is carefully considered, so athletes perform at the very top of their games. Great athletes turn away from bad food. They turn away from people or things that keep them from being the great athletes they are.

Christians must have that same resolve about spiritual things. Paul says, "for the training of the body has a limited benefit, but godliness is beneficial in every way, since it holds promise for the present life and also for the life to come" (1 Tim. 4:8). Godly people do their best to turn from sin.

# Roll up your sleeves

While we're on the topic of sports, let me ask you a couple of questions. How did Lebron James get so good at basketball? How did Giancarlo Stanton become such a great homerun hitter? They practice! This is not to say they didn't begin with an athletic edge. Lebron and Giancarlo are giant men. But both have been diligent to perfect their games through the years.

Giancarlo takes thousands of practice swings a year. Lebron shoots thousands of shots in practice each year. All these practices prepare them for the game. Christians are people who practice communing with God. Reading the Word of God, praying to the Lord, and attending church are all ways for us to prepare to resist the temptations we are going to face each day.

If you were to skip all your practices before the baseball season, would you be surprised to strike out in the first game? You shouldn't be. You didn't take the time to get ready for the game. You didn't take the time to find the right bat or work on your timing. You simply weren't ready, and you failed.

Being a disciple of Jesus is about being disciplined in life. You can see that the word "disciple" is related to the word "discipline." It's prideful for us to think we can handle temptation without discipline in reading God's Word, fellowship with other Christians, and perseverance in our prayer lives. In order to live lives of repentance, we must humble ourselves, trust the work of God's Spirit in us, and work hard toward becoming more like Jesus.

John Newton said, "Lord give me a humbling sense of my sins, give me a humbling view of thy glory, give me a humbling view of thy love, for surely nothing humbles like these."[4] Ask God to break your heart over your sin. Ask God to give you insight into his beauty. Ask God to help you better understand his great love for you. All these things will help you turn from sin.

The great Reformer Martin Luther wrote these words in his song, "A Mighty Fortress is our God":

Did we in our own strength confide,

our striving would be losing,

Were not the right Man on our side,

the Man of God's own choosing:

Do you ask who that may be? Christ Jesus, it is He;

Lord of Armies, His Name, from age to age the same

And He must win the battle.

Remember, young Christian: We are to "produce fruit in keeping with repentance."

# Questions to consider

1. Do you have the fruit of repentance in your life? Do you admit and turn from sin?

2. What kind of fruit comes from a lemon tree? What kind of fruit does a Christian produce?

3. Are you disciplining yourself with the Word of God and prayer? Are you faithfully attending church?

4. What are the sins that you need to turn from right now?

5. Are there people from whom you need to ask forgiveness?

# Truths to remember

1. The Christian life is hard work!

2. Athletes have to practice to be ready for the game.

3. It's very important to read God's Word.

4. Pray for God to give you the strength to endure temptation, the humble attitude to take responsibility when you fail, and willingness to repent (turn) when you sin.

# Memory Verses

**SIGHT OF SIN:** "No discipline seems enjoyable at the time, but painful. Later on, however, it yields the fruit of peace and righteousness to those who have been trained by it" (Heb. 12:11).

**SORROW FOR SIN:** "For I am conscious of my rebellion, and my sin is always before me" (Ps. 51:3).

**CONFESSION OF SIN:** "If we confess our sins, He is faithful and righteous to forgive us our sins and to cleanse us from all unrighteousness" (1 John 1:9).

**SHAME OF SIN:** "... keeping our eyes on Jesus, the source and perfecter of our faith, who for the joy that lay before Him endured a cross and despised the shame and has sat down at the right hand of God's throne" (Heb. 12:2).

**HATRED OF SIN:** "For the wages of sin is death, but the gift of God is eternal life in Christ Jesus our Lord" (Rom. 6:23).

**TURNING FROM SIN:** "Therefore produce fruit consistent with repentance" (Matt. 3:8).

# PART 4 | What Is Justification?

By Martin Winslow

## Don't we all want justice?

I didn't deserve to be in the principal's office; I hadn't done anything wrong. I was in trouble because I was in the wrong place at the wrong time. A bunch of guys were throwing spitballs in class, and I had been sitting next to them. When the teacher turned around and saw a spitball fly through the air, I, along with a couple of guys around me, were sent to see the principal. I was innocent, yet called guilty. Is there anything worse?

Have you ever been falsely accused of something? If it hasn't happened to you yet, just wait; at some point, it probably will. None of us likes to be accused or punished for something we didn't do. In fact, if we're punished for something we didn't do, the one who punished us is acting unjustly. We want to be treated justly, don't we?

That may be more of a tricky question than you think. Let me ask you a slightly different question: Would you want God to give you justice for the sins you have committed? If God dealt with your sins and punished you for them, you would be in a lot of trouble.

God is holy and perfect. He is so holy that James, the brother of Jesus, says, "For whoever keeps the entire law, yet fails in one point, is guilty of breaking it all" (Jas. 2:10). This means if you only sinned once, it's just like being guilty of breaking all of God's commands.

So, what would be the outcome of our sin if God dealt justly with us? We would go to hell. Hell is a place where sin is punished for eternity.

Eternity means forever and ever. Because God is perfect, his own character demands that we pay for every sin. Now, let me ask you again: Do you want justice for yourself?

Thankfully, because of God's grace, there's a way for him to satisfy his justice without sending us to hell. The cross of Jesus makes our rescue secure, and that's what justification is all about. "Justification" is a very important term, and this part of the book will explain in further detail just how it works. I recommend that parents read through one chapter a night with their kids and talk through the "Questions to consider" and "Truths to remember."

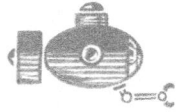

# PART 4.1 | Wages and Gifts

MEMORY VERSE - ROM. 6:23
"For the wages of sin is death, but the gift of God
is eternal life in Christ Jesus our Lord."

## Wages are earned

Have you ever done a job for someone and, after completing it, you got paid? Did it make you feel good to receive money for the hard work you did? The payment you received was the wage you earned for completing the job. Earning something in that way feels good.

I remember, as a kid, mowing lawns all afternoon in the hot sun. When I was finished, I would go up to the door of the house, and someone would put that hard-earned cash in my hand. That felt the best! Many times, I would go down to the Casey's or 7-Eleven and buy a Slurpee to cool off. Buying that Slurpee with my own money felt great.

In the spiritual realm, you also earn a wage for the work of sin. The wage you earn for this work is death. It doesn't feel quite as good to earn this type of wage, does it? You're in good company, or rather, bad company. Romans 3:10 says, "There is no one righteous, not even one." Every person to walk the earth has earned death.

Well, almost every person. There was one person who never sinned, and because of that good news, you and I have hope. Jesus said, "Don't assume that I came to destroy the Law or the Prophets. I did not come to destroy but to fulfill" (Matt. 5:17).

The law that you and I broke, Jesus fulfilled, or kept, perfectly. That, of course, is good news for Jesus, but you may wonder how that relates to you and me. Before we get to that answer, we need to talk about how we got into this sin mess.

# Is sin my fault, or Adam and Eve's fault?

YES! You might think, if our first parents (Adam and Eve) are to blame for this "sin thing," maybe we aren't accountable to God after all. In truth, Adam and Eve *are* guilty, and so are you. To sin means to "miss the mark." Adam, Eve, you, I, and everyone we know have missed the mark of God's holy standard found in his Word.

There are more than six hundred laws mentioned in the Old Testament. Let's just look at the ten most famous laws, found in Exodus 20, and see if we have ever broken any of these:

1. You shall have no other gods before me [God].
2. You shall not make for yourself any carved image.
3. You shall not take the name of the Lord your God in vain.
4. Remember the Sabbath Day to keep it holy.
5. Honor your father and your mother.
6. You shall not murder.
7. You shall not commit adultery.
8. You shall not steal.
9. You shall not lie.
10. You shall not covet.

You're not alone. Every single human being is in the same place. Sin is the fault of all of us. While Adam and Eve were the persons through whom sin entered the world, we are born not only with their guilt, but with guilt for the sins we commit as soon we get the chance.

Romans 5:12 says, "Therefore, just as sin entered the world through one man, and death through sin, in this way death spread to all men, because all sinned." Notice the last phrase, "because all sinned." We did it to ourselves. This sin brings death.

It would be horrible if the verse were the final say, but it isn't. Notice the memory verse for this chapter: "For the wages of sin is death, but the gift of God is eternal life in Christ Jesus our Lord" (Rom. 6:23). The bad news is sin and death, but the good news is the gift of eternal life.

# Gifts are free

The gift of eternal life is not like the wage of death you earned. A gift is a thing given willingly to someone without payment. My favorite time of the year is Christmas. Every year, when we celebrate the birth of Christ, we place gifts under a Christmas tree. Gifts we receive aren't things we worked hard for and received because we earned them, like wages for mowing a lawn. They are given to us freely out of love from the person who bought and wrapped them for us.

We receive Christmas gifts whether our behavior is good or bad. They are gifts; nothing is expected in return for them. We don't pay for these presents or do anything to earn them.

Now, think about it: the gift of God is eternal life in Christ. This means you do not, and cannot, earn eternal life. It's a gift. It's free and there for us to take. The gift of God is therefore different than the wages of sin. So, what exactly is the gift Jesus gives to his children?

Remember how we just saw ten of God's commandments and realized that we're sinners? Jesus not only kept these commands perfectly; he also kept perfectly every command God ever spoke. This active obedience by Jesus to all of God's laws made him completely righteous before God. This righteousness he gives to us freely as a gift when we trust him by faith.

This gift doesn't mean we become righteous. It means we who trust Jesus are covered by Jesus' righteousness. We remain sinful people, but the perfect and finished work of Christ has been credited to our accounts.

Hebrews 10:14 says it this way: "For by one offering He has perfected forever those who are sanctified." Jesus' sacrifice on the cross in the place of sinners is not a wage we can earn, but a gift God bestows, free of charge, upon all who believe. It seems strange to receive the gift of forgiveness, a relationship with God, and heaven for eternity completely free; yet, this is exactly what the Scriptures teach.

# Questions to consider

1. Do you ever feel you must earn God's favor? Do you really have to do this?

2. Have you admitted in your heart that you have broken God's laws?

3. Do you believe Jesus kept all of God's laws perfectly?

4. Can you explain the difference between a wage and a gift?

# Truths to remember

1. We are guilty of sin, not only because of Adam and Eve, but because of our own sin.

2. Eternal life is a gift from God. It cannot be earned. All you must do is trust in Jesus' perfect life in your place, his death that you deserved, and his resurrection that proves everything he said is true.

# PART 4.2 | Trouble in the Courtroom

## MEMORY VERSE - ROM. 3:10
"… as it is written: There is no one righteous, not even one."

Have you ever been to a courtroom? Maybe you've seen one on TV. In a courtroom, a complaint is brought against someone. This complaint is brought by a person called a plaintiff. He brings his case against someone he claims has done him wrong. The person the plaintiff is complaining against is trying to defend himself, so, he is known as the defendant.

The most important person in the room is the one who gets to make the final decision regarding the complaint. She's the judge. She either decides the defendant is guilty of doing wrong and punishes him, or she determines the defendant is right and the plaintiff is wrong. In this case, the defendant is released.

If all your past decisions were recorded and played back in front of God, would God find you sinful or perfect? We all know the answer to that question. The Bible says "there is no one righteous, not even one" (Rom. 3:10). If our whole lives were played back on a huge screen in front of God, we know that we would be embarrassed and found guilty of many sins.

Imagine for a minute what would happen inside a courtroom if our sins were taken into account against us.

# The judge: God

We know some things about the judge. The judge is perfect. Scripture says, "God — His way is perfect …" (Ps. 18:30). God is also holy. This word means "set apart." It also contains the idea of being different or "other." God is perfect in all his ways and set apart from the things he has created. He made man, in his original goodness, to be perfect and to enjoy fellowship with him.

At the Fall, humans fell from perfection and out of this relationship. Because of our rebellion against the laws of God, we will appear before the judge, bearing all our sins. His expectation is for us to be set apart and holy, as he is. In 1 Peter 1:16, we read, "Be holy, because I am holy." The judge in the heavenly courtroom (God) demands perfection of his creatures.

Are you ready to meet the judge of the universe? He is perfect, he is holy, and he demands the same from you and me. But we cannot live up to this. We aren't perfect. So, how can we meet the demands of our righteous judge?

It's important to remember that God, the judge, is not only perfect; he's also merciful. In the Ten Commandments, after saying, "Do not make an idol for yourself ..." he goes on to say, "I, the LORD your God, am a jealous God, punishing the children for the fathers' sin, to the third and fourth generations of those who hate Me, but showing faithful love to a thousand generations of those who love Me and keep My commands" (Ex. 20:4-6).

Lovingkindness is extended from the judge to those who love and obey him. The problem is, we can't always keep his commandments, and the judge knows it.

# The prosecution: God's law

In this courtroom, the prosecutor accusing you is God's law. We know some things about the prosecutor. The prosecutor is out to make a case against you. His job is to prove your guilt. I already mentioned the evidence that the prosecutor has against you. The evidence is all the laws God gave us in the Bible, which we have broken. Every time we lie, steal, covet, or dishonor God or our parents, we break God's law.

This prosecutor comes to the perfect judge. He tells the judge how you have broken the laws repeatedly. He recounts your sins from the time you were tiny. Many of them you had forgotten, but you now remember the accusations as true. He tells about the bickering with your siblings last week. He tells the judge about the first time you lied. He tells stories of when you didn't honor your mother and father, and when you were greedy and selfish.

The prosecution easily demonstrates that you are a guilty person. Not only are you embarrassed, but you are also in a lot of trouble with the judge.

# The defendant: you

After the prosecutor is finished listing the sins you have committed, you know you are in big trouble. What do you deserve for all your broken promises, your bad behavior, and your rebellion against the truth? Remember the verse cited earlier: "For the wages of sin is death ..." (Rom. 6:23)? Even sinful thoughts deserve death. If your sins were recounted in front of this judge and courtroom, you would feel like Adam and Eve did. You would want to hide and cover up the shame and guilt that everyone had seen.

It's hard to believe that every one of your sins is known by God, isn't it? Yet, the Bible tells us that God knows even the small details going on in the world, even the number of hairs on your head. Jesus also says, "Aren't two sparrows sold for a penny? Yet not one of them falls to the ground without your Father's consent" (Matt. 10:29). Not even a bird dies without God knowing about it. We know we are guilty, because God knows all our weaknesses.

Jeremiah 17:10 says, "I, Yahweh, examine the mind, I test the heart to give to each according to his way, according to what his actions deserve." Wow! He can read our minds. No sin escapes God.

# Trouble in the courtroom

The law of God has shown that you and I are sinners and have broken God's laws. Because of this, the holy, perfect judge (God) looks at us and tells us to stand up as he renders his verdict. The judge says:

> The court finds the defendant (you) guilty of sin. The punishment for this sin is physical and spiritual death. When you die, you will be separated from me for eternity in a place of torment called hell. In this place, you will suffer for your sins and be separated from my kindness. There will be no joy in hell. There will be no love in hell. There will never be a chance to leave hell. It will be eternal punishment.

When a verdict is handed down, there's a final raising of the gavel. When the gavel is slammed down on the judge's bench, the decision is final. Your sentence has been read. Now, the judge raises the gavel, preparing to slam it down.

# Questions to consider

1. Do you realize that God knows all your sins? How does that make you feel?

2. What does it mean that God is the perfect judge?

3. What does the prosecutor have against each of us?

4. Who is the defendant in the story above? Do you have a good defense for your sins?

# Truths to remember

1. God is holy and perfect, and he expects the same from us.

2. You aren't holy and perfect. You're a sinner, and this means you deserve death.

3. What's going to happen to you if the gavel is slammed down in the above story?

# PART 4.3 | Mercy in the Courtroom

### MEMORY VERSES - ROM. 8:1-2
"Therefore, no condemnation now exists for those in Christ Jesus, because the Spirit's law of life in Christ Jesus has set you free from the law of sin and of death."

## Justice and mercy

If that gavel slammed down, where would you go for eternity when you die? If you were found guilty of your sins, you would be without any hope of escaping the law of God, the perfect judge who gave the law. You would be sent to eternal punishment. Thankfully, this does not have to happen.

God, the judge, is not only perfect and holy, but also kind and compassionate. God's desire is for people to be reconciled with him. God has shown himself to be a God of great mercy. James 2:13 says, "For judgment is without mercy to the one who hasn't shown mercy. Mercy triumphs over judgment." Mercy triumphs over judgment!

## Good news

What if, right before the judge slammed down his gavel, someone came into the room and yelled, "Stop"? And what if, when the judge heard this, he immediately stopped to listen? This person said he would like to take on the guilt and punishment for your sin. This person did not deserve punishment and death, because he has kept all God's laws perfectly. The person went on to say that he would like to use all his perfection to cover your imperfection. He would willingly die in your place to set you free.

Does this sound familiar? Of course it does. Jesus tells us in the Sermon on the Mount:

Don't assume that I came to destroy the Law or the Prophets. I did not come to destroy but to fulfill. For I assure you: Until heaven and earth pass away, not the smallest letter or one stroke of a letter will pass from the law until all things are accomplished (Matt. 5:17-18).

Jesus is saying that all of God's laws were perfectly fulfilled through the life of Jesus. He lived a life of complete perfection. This makes him qualified to stand before the law and not be prosecuted. There are no accusations from God's law that can be brought against Jesus. He stands before the perfect judge, perfect himself.

This is the gospel story we read in the New Testament. The word "gospel" means "good news." The good news is that you don't have to suffer for your sins. Christ has willingly done that in your place on the cross. The memory verse above says, "Therefore, no condemnation now exists for those in Christ Jesus ...." (Rom. 8:1).

"Condemnation" comes from two Greek words and literally means "judgment against." There is no judgment against those who are in Christ Jesus. Those who have trusted in Jesus are not judged by God, but judgment for their sins fell on Christ in his suffering, crucifixion, and death. Not only did Jesus take our sins upon himself; he allowed us to borrow his righteousness. I will explain more about this in the next chapter.

# No judgment for me at all?

We see in 2 Corinthians 5:10, "For we must all appear before the tribunal of Christ, so that each may be repaid for what he has done in the body, whether good or worthless." Didn't Jesus say, that whoever believes in him has passed from judgment to life? Is the Bible contradicting itself?

Not at all. All judgment for our sins has fallen on Jesus. Among Jesus' last words on the cross was this one: *tetelestai*. This Greek word means "paid in full." When the verse in 2 Corinthians says we will appear and be judged, this judgment is for rewards given to Christians.

The judgment seat in Greek is *bema*. The *bema* is where awards were given to people during ancient Roman times. Imagine athletes being rewarded during the Isthmian Games, which occurred in Corinth and were similar to the Olympics in Athens. The winners stand on boxes. On the top box is the gold medalist, the lower right is silver, and the lower left is bronze. Each receives an award based on what he accomplished.

The same will be done for Christians at the end. Rewards will be given according to what each has done. So, yes, Christians will be judged. But it is not a judgment that leads to punishment. Your punishment was taken care of at the cross. If you're a Christian, your final judgment is for reward.

The useless things we have done with our lives are burned up, as in a fire, according to 1 Corinthians 3. All our bad deeds were put on the cross, and all that's left for our judgment is what Paul calls "gold, silver, costly stones" (1 Cor. 3:12). The precious things Christians have done will be weighed and rewarded. The other stuff was paid for at the cross of Christ. In Romans 2, Paul talks about the difference between judgment for a non-Christian in verses 5-9, and then judgment for a Christian in verses 10-11:

> But because of your hardness and unrepentant heart you are storing up wrath for yourself in the day of wrath, when God's righteous judgment is revealed. He will repay each one according to his works: eternal life to those who by persistence in doing good seek glory, honor, and immortality; but wrath and indignation to those who are self-seeking and disobey the truth but are obeying unrighteousness; affliction and distress for every human being who does evil, first to the Jew, and also to the Greek; but glory, honor, and peace for everyone who does what is good, first to the Jew, and also to the Greek. There is no favoritism with God.

Jesus said, "I assure you: Anyone who hears My word and believes Him who sent Me has eternal life and will not come under judgment but has passed from death to life" (John 5:24). Isn't that amazing news? Christ did everything for you.

# Trust the gospel!

Many times during your life, you will feel unworthy to be a Christian. You will feel like your sin is too much for God to forgive, and you will question whether you are a Christian. Remember, during these moments of doubt, that you are unworthy of heaven. You don't deserve heaven or a relationship with God.

But also remind yourself that Jesus gave you the gift of salvation, free and undeserved. He gives you mercy, and not because you deserve it. He gives you mercy because your punishment was given to Jesus, and Jesus' goodness covers you. The gospel is about what God has done for you, not about what you can do for God.

# Questions to consider

1. What would happen if God judged you based on your works rather than on Jesus' works?

2. Who took your place in the courtroom? Have you accepted this truth in your life?

3. The Greek word for condemnation can be translated as two words. What are they?

4. Is there any judgment against people who trust in Christ's death in their place?

5. Hebrews 9:27 says, "And just as it is appointed for people to die once — and after this, judgment ...." Are you prepared for your judgment?

# Truths to remember

1. You don't deserve God's mercy. It's a gift!

2. Christians will be judged. But their judgment will be one in which they are rewarded.

3. Non-Christians will be judged for their sins and will be condemned to hell.

4. We bring nothing to God that is worthy of salvation. We deserve wrath and punishment, but because of Christ's kindness, we receive mercy and grace.

# PART 4.4 | Captain America's Shield

## MEMORY VERSES - ROM. 8:3-4

"What the law could not do since it was limited by the flesh, God did. He condemned sin in the flesh by sending His own Son in flesh like ours under sin's domain, and as a sin offering, in order that the law's requirement would be accomplished in us who do not walk according to the flesh but according to the Spirit."

Captain America's weapon of choice is his shield. It's made from a special metal that renders it impenetrable. If you were going to be attacked in "comic world," and Captain America threw you his shield for protection, you would be saved from the enemy. His shield would protect you. If he loaned you his shield, it would also make him vulnerable to the attack that had been coming at you.

Now pay attention to this part: God demands perfection from human beings. Because we can't meet this requirement, the judgment of God is coming to each one of us. But for those of us who have trusted in Christ, we use the righteousness of Christ as our shield. It protects us from the wrath we deserve for breaking the laws of God. Jesus then leaves himself unprotected and takes upon himself our sin by dying on the cross.

Justification is Jesus giving us his righteous deeds to use as a shield, while leaving himself vulnerable and taking our judgment. We didn't earn this kindness from Jesus. It's simply a gift we receive by faith.

In the story above, when I used Captain America's shield, it didn't become my shield. I am borrowing his shield, and because I have it, I am protected from the bad guy, Red Skull, or whoever else I might be fighting in the comic world.

God the Father, who is the righteous judge, looks at Christ's perfect works. Based on those works, which remain his but cover us, God doesn't punish us. Christ's works are like the impenetrable shield. They are perfect works we borrow, and God is pleased to loan them to us.

Jesus took upon himself the punishment we deserve. All the wrath for sin and unrighteous deeds was placed upon him at the cross. The work of God justifying us, based on the works of Christ, doesn't magically change us. Instead, we become outwardly protected from the wrath of God we deserve. Jesus took that wrath on the cross and saved us from it. Jesus gave us his good works and paid for our bad works.

# Double imputation

If you hit a double in baseball, it means you get to second base. "Double" means "two." You get two bases with a double. Double imputation means two things were happening at one time when Jesus died on the cross.

The first thing that happened was that our guilt was credited to Jesus. Jesus paid the price for the sins of all Christians on the cross. The second thing that happened was that Christ's righteousness was credited to us. All Jesus' perfect deeds were credited to our accounts, and God was satisfied.

For Christians, Jesus suffered the consequences of the sin debt we owed God. The wrath we deserved was poured out upon him. Jesus did not become a sinner on the cross. Jesus became a sin offering on the cross. You did not become a perfect person at the cross. You received the perfect righteousness of Jesus credited to your account at the cross.

Consider this verse: "He made the One who did not know sin to be sin for us, so that we might become the righteousness of God in Him" (2 Cor. 5:21).

# The onion on the stick

When I was a teenager, my church youth group had a party. One of the games our youth minister had us play involved a huge tray of caramel apples. He lined up ten willing and excited students. The game was to see who could eat a caramel apple fastest. The winner would get a gift certificate. We were all excited to see who was going to win. Finally, he yelled out, "Go!"

Everyone quickly began to bite into the caramel apples and then immediately started spitting out their "apples" and running to the bathrooms and water fountains. It was a trick! Many of the caramel apples weren't caramel apples at all, but caramel-covered onions. The students were disgusted to bite into raw onions rather than the sweet apples they expected.

Christians are kind of like that caramel-covered onion. The beautiful, wonderful, perfect works of Christ are like that delicious caramel on the outside. It's pleasing, sweet, and amazing. Underneath is a nasty raw onion. We are the onions, and the perfect works of Jesus are the caramel.

When Luther said we are "fully just" before God, he meant that we are covered by the perfect works of Jesus. When he said that we are also "fully sinful at the same time," he reminded us that the old sinful persons we are still exist under those works of Christ.

Even though the perfection of Christ covers us, we still are the children of our sinful parents, Adam and Eve. This means that we will never be able to keep all of God's laws. Our flesh is weak and sinful. As our memory passage for this chapter reads, "What the law could not do since it was limited by the flesh, God did. He condemned sin in the flesh by sending His own Son in flesh like ours under sin's domain, and as a sin offering" (Rom. 8:3).

We human beings are too weak to keep the law perfectly. But God sent Jesus, the God-Man, to die for our sins and pay the price for them with his life. The rest of the memory passage says, "... in order that the law's requirement would be accomplished in us who do not walk according to the flesh but according to the Spirit" (Rom. 8:4).

The perfection God's law demanded from us is fulfilled when we repent of our sins and believe in Jesus' death, burial, and resurrection on our behalf. When we do this, the onion that is us is covered by that sweet caramel of Christ's righteous deeds. Now, when God the Father looks at you, he doesn't see the onion (your old sinful self), but instead sees the caramel (the perfect works of Christ).

# Questions to consider

1. Does it help you to think of Christ's perfect works as a shield?

2. Did you realize that Christ, giving you his righteous works as a shield, is left with your sins and unprotected?

3. Are you as grateful to God as you should be for what he did for you on the cross?

# Truths to remember

1. "Justification" does not mean you're not a sinner anymore. Remember, you are like the onion under the caramel. You're still a sinner. You're just covered by Christ's goodness.

2. "Double imputation" means that two things happened at one time at the cross. Christ's righteousness was credited to us, and our guilt was credited to Jesus. He rescued us!

# PART 4.5 | A Life of Thanksgiving

MEMORY VERSE - COL. 2:14
"He erased the certificate of debt, with its obligations, that was against us and opposed to us, and has taken it out of the way by nailing it to the cross."

## Would you be thankful?

If I bought you the thing you've always wanted, would you be grateful? What if you were about to be hit by a car, and I jumped in front of it and saved your life? What would you think of me? God, in his grace, gave you his life. He died a horrible death on the cross to give you and me life with him. Are you grateful? If so, does your life demonstrate that?

The grace that God gives us is not cheap. Our gift of salvation cost Jesus everything. Paul says to the Corinthian church in 1 Corinthians 6:20, "for you were bought at a price. Therefore glorify God in your body." In other words, we owe Jesus our bodies, because he bought us by giving his body in our place on the cross.

Christian martyr Dietrich Bonhoeffer once said, "Such grace is costly because it calls us to follow, and it is grace because it calls us to follow Jesus Christ. It is costly because it costs a man his life, and it is grace because it gives a man the only true life. It is costly because it condemns sin, and grace because it justifies the sinner."[1] We will escape that wrath and receive what Christ deserves, eternal blessing and honor.

There is a famous song, "Jesus Paid It All." The chorus says:
> Jesus paid it all,
> all to him I owe,
> sin had left a crimson stain,
> he washed it white as snow.

Are you thankful to God for what he has done for you?

# The proper response to God's grace

Some might say, since we have been forgiven of our sins, it doesn't matter how we live. Jesus has paid the price for all my sins; therefore, I am free to live as I see fit. They may go on to say that we are not saved by our good deeds, so it doesn't matter what we do, or how we do it. If anyone says these things, they have not realized that the gospel transforms a person's life, inside and out.

It is true that we are not saved by any of our good deeds. But it is also true that we are saved "unto good deeds." Ephesians 2:8-10 describes salvation well:

> For you are saved by grace through faith, and this is not from yourselves; it is God's gift — not from works, so that no one can boast. For we are His creation, created in Christ Jesus for good works, which God prepared ahead of time so that we should walk in them.

This passage says we are saved by grace, through our faith, which is a gift from God. This passage also goes on to say that we are "created in Christ Jesus for good works." It *does* matter how we live. We can't just say we are forgiven and do whatever we want. We are called to live lives that demonstrate our thankfulness to God for what he has done for us.

Paul writes in Romans 6:1-2, "What should we say then? Should we continue in sin so that grace may multiply? Absolutely not! How can we who died to sin still live in it?"

Our response to Jesus graciously taking our place on the cross should not be to continue in our sin as if it means nothing; but instead, we should live as best we can to please God. God has given his Spirit to dwell in us. His Spirit comforts us when we need it, and convicts us of sin when we need that. Our proper response to God's grace should be lives that strive to be holy.

When we do mess up, we have God's safety net of grace there to catch us. As 1 John 2:1-2 says:

My little children, I am writing you these things so that you may not sin. But if anyone does sin, we have an advocate with the Father — Jesus Christ the Righteous One. He Himself is the propitiation for our sins, and not only for ours, but also for those of the whole world.

Notice that John says he's writing to church members so they will not sin. Sin is a big deal, and Christians are to flee from it. After healing the man at the pool called Bethesda in John 5:14, Jesus warns him, "Do not sin anymore, so that something worse doesn't happen to you." He also tells the woman caught in adultery, after he had forgiven her, "Go and sin no more" (John 8:11).

Our proper response to Christ's sacrifice and forgiveness is to repent and turn from sin. When Zacchaeus believed in Jesus, do you remember what he said? "But Zacchaeus stood there and said to the Lord, 'Look, I'll give half of my possessions to the poor, Lord! And if I have extorted anything from anyone, I'll pay back four times as much!'" (Luke 19:8). Grace led Zacchaeus to obedience, not disobedience.

However, our flesh is weak, and we do mess up. It is during these times we remember 1 John 2:1, "if anyone does sin, we have an advocate with the Father — Jesus Christ the Righteous One." An advocate is someone who fights in your corner. Jesus fought sin and death for you and defeated both. Because of him, you are totally forgiven. He is your advocate, fighting in your corner!

# Thankful in every situation

Fanny Crosby was born March 24, 1820. When she was born, she had an eye infection. Her parents sought help from someone who smeared a paste in her eyes. Unfortunately, the paste blinded Fanny. Even though, early on, she lost the ability to see, she was still a very happy and thankful child. At just eight years old, she wrote this poem:

Oh, what a happy child I am, although I cannot see,
I am resolved that in this world contented I will be.
How many blessings I enjoy that other people don't,
So, weep or sigh because I'm blind, I cannot nor – I won't.[2]

Fanny's blindness did not keep her from enjoying a life full of God's blessings. It also didn't keep her from living a life of thankfulness to God. Fanny realized all Christ had done for her, and that caused her to not concentrate on her blindness, but instead to love and adore the God with whom she would spend eternity. Instead of being caught up in the difficulties of blindness, Fanny concentrated on the love of God she experienced in the gospel.

When we realize that our sins mean we deserve to be eternally separated from God, yet the cross rescued us from this fate, it should move us to love God with our whole hearts. No matter what our difficulties, we are guaranteed a relationship with God forever through Christ's death, burial, and resurrection.

There's an old song that says:
> Turn your eyes upon Jesus,
> look full in His wonderful face,
> and the things of earth will grow strangely dim
> in the light of His glory and grace.

When we understand the gospel, we know we can face any of life's difficulties because we will spend eternity with God. If you have believed the gospel, there's no longer a judgment against you. You have been justified completely and no longer held accountable for your sins.

In all of life's difficulties, you must remember the important truth that, in God's courtroom, your judgment fell upon Jesus, and his goodness fell upon you. Because this is true, remember Paul's words in 1 Thessalonians 5:18, "Give thanks in everything, for this is God's will for you in Christ Jesus."

## Questions to consider

1. Are you truly thankful for what Jesus did for you on the cross?

2. What is the proper response to God's goodness?

3. Since Jesus paid the price for all our sins, is it okay for us to just go on sinning? Why or why not?

# Truths to remember

1. On several occasions, Jesus warned people about sin, including the man he healed at the Pool of Bethesda and the woman caught in adultery.

2. The grace that God gives us should not be taken lightly; it cost Jesus his life. We should take his commands and his sacrifice for us seriously.

3. Why should we be thankful in every circumstance? Why is Fanny Crosby a good example of this?

# Memory Verses

**WAGES AND GIFTS:** "For the wages of sin is death, but the gift of God is eternal life in Christ Jesus our Lord" (Rom. 6:23).

**TROUBLE IN THE COURTROOM:** "... as it is written: There is no one righteous, not even one" (Rom. 3:10).

**MERCY IN THE COURTROOM:** "Therefore, no condemnation now exists for those in Christ Jesus, because the Spirit's law of life in Christ Jesus has set you free from the law of sin and of death" (Rom. 8:1-2).

**CAPTAIN AMERICA'S SHIELD:** "What the law could not do since it was limited by the flesh, God did. He condemned sin in the flesh by sending His own Son in flesh like ours under sin's domain, and as a sin offering, in order that the law's requirement would be accomplished in us who do not walk according to the flesh but according to the Spirit" (Rom. 8:3-4).

**A LIFE OF THANKSGIVING:** "He erased the certificate of debt, with its obligations, that was against us and opposed to us, and has taken it out of the way by nailing it to the cross" (Col. 2:14).

# PART 5 | What Is Faith?

By Brad Delaughter & Martin Winslow

Every time I (Martin) get ready to board an airplane, my stomach turns a little. I can't help but wonder how the plane gets off the ground with so much weight inside. I worry about something going wrong. It doesn't seem we ought to be able to go 550 miles per hour at 37,000 feet. Statistically, traveling by plane is far safer than riding in a car. But it's crazy to think that man is able to fly.

When I decide to board the plane, I'm putting my faith in things that are out of my control to get to a place I want to go. By stepping onto the plane, I'm taking a step of faith that I believe I will end up at my destination.

In order to have faith and board the plane, I don't have to understand the physics of how the plane gets into the air. I don't have to understand the ratio of engine thrust to wind drag. All I have to do is believe, trust, and obey.

Like flying in an airplane, we exercise faith every day in the simple things of life. When we get sick, we have faith that the doctor who gave us medicine is competent. We believe the doctor gave us the right medicine, and we trust that the doctor's knowledge of medicine prepared him or her to prescribe it accurately. After this, we obey what they told us to do by taking the medicine.

Those three elements of belief, trust, and obedience largely comprise what faith in the gospel of Jesus Christ looks like. Don't make the mistake of thinking that Christian faith is simply holding to a few propositional truths the way we might believe vanilla ice cream tastes good, the sun is hot, or $2 + 2 = 4$. Biblical faith is much more than affirming propositions.

Biblical faith is practiced by those who have been changed by the gospel. Biblical faith has substance to it.

The New Testament Greek word for faith is *pisteuo.* This word is dynamic to cover the ideas of belief, trust, and obedience.

The answer to Question 21 of The Heidelberg Catechism — "What is saving faith?" — provides perhaps the clearest description of saving faith found in any confession:

> True faith is not only sure knowledge, whereby I hold for truth all that God has revealed to us in His Word, but also firm confidence which the Holy Spirit works in my heart by the gospel, that not only to others, but to me also, remission of sins, everlasting righteousness and salvation are freely given by God, merely of grace, only for the sake of Christ's merits.[1]

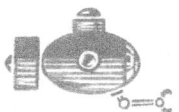

# PART 5.1 | Faith Is Believing

## MEMORY VERSE - JOHN 3:16

"For God loved the world in this way: He gave His One and Only Son, so that everyone who believes in Him will not perish but have eternal life."

## Believing

If a good friend told you there was an incredible new ice cream shop that opened five miles from your house, would you believe him? How would you investigate to find out if it were true?

Before you believe it, you might ask where the shop is located. You might ask about nearby landmarks. Then you might ask your friend when he went there, who was with him, and what kind of ice cream he had. If he answered all of these questions well, you might get excited, believing your friend has told you the truth about this great new place.

Finally, you tell your parents about this new restaurant, jump in the car, and experience it for yourself. Your belief in the words of your friend led to you try out the new shop. After you eat ice cream at the new shop, you realize that everything your friend told you is true, and you experienced it for yourself.

Every day, we're challenged with new things to believe. Your teachers present you with information about science, history, math, and other subjects that you are expected to believe. Your parents, grandparents, and church leaders tell you stories of things that happened in the past, and you are expected to believe them.

But how do you know that the things everyone is telling you are true? How do you know the story of Jesus is true? Was he really born of a virgin? Did he truly die for the sins of the world and rise again three days later? How do you know you can believe this story?

# We need evidence!

How can I believe Jesus will save me if I don't know first that he was able to save himself? If he was crucified on a Roman cross and buried, how do I know that he actually rose from the dead?

The historical biblical evidence that Jesus rose from the dead is strong. At least ten times in the Gospels and the Book of Acts, we see that Jesus is risen from the dead. Numerous appearances of Jesus are referenced, including Jesus appearing to over 500 people at one time (1 Cor. 15:6).

One of the most compelling scenes from the Gospels is the story of Thomas, one of Jesus' disciples. Thomas told his friends, "If I don't see the mark of the nails in His hands, put my finger into the mark of the nails, and put my hand into His side, I will never believe!" (John 20:25). Thomas needed evidence of Jesus' resurrection. He wasn't going to blindly believe a Savior that he hadn't seen save himself. This challenge of Thomas would not go unanswered.

The Bible goes on, in John 20:26-29, to tell us the rest of the story:

> After eight days His disciples were indoors again, and Thomas was with them. Even though the doors were locked, Jesus came and stood among them. He said, "Peace to you!" Then He said to Thomas, "Put your finger here and observe My hands. Reach out your hand and put it into My side. Don't be an unbeliever, but a believer." Thomas responded to Him, "My Lord and my God!" Jesus said, "Because you have seen Me, you have believed. Those who believe without seeing are blessed."

You may be thinking, somewhat skeptically, that this is just what the Bible says. How can I believe that the event of Jesus' resurrection is really a historical event?

# Minimal facts

Some historians try to deny the historical claims of Christianity. They speak as if Jesus' followers made up the major tenets of Christianity; thus, neither the New Testament nor its claims can be trusted. Years ago, New

Testament scholar and philosopher Gary Habermas developed what he called the "minimal facts argument" regarding the resurrection of Jesus.

Here's how it works: Habermas consulted scholarship outside the New Testament to prove his case. He scanned accepted historical literature from the first couple of centuries AD. He went to non-religious, atheist, and agnostic sources. The source didn't matter, so long as it was not biblical. He consulted these sources for early testimony about Jesus.

Habermas concluded six minimal facts from early non-believers. These facts include the following: 1) Jesus died by crucifixion; 2) very soon afterwards, his followers had real experiences that they believed were actual appearances of the risen Jesus; 3) the lives of these followers were transformed as a result, even to the point of being willing to die specifically for their faith in the resurrection message; 4) these things were taught very early, soon after the crucifixion; 5) James, Jesus' unbelieving brother, became a Christian due to his own experience with the resurrected Christ; and 6) the Christian persecutor Paul (formerly Saul of Tarsus) became a believer after a similar experience.[2]

# Do you believe?

Do you believe in the death, burial, and resurrection of Jesus for the remission of your sins? If you don't, you cannot be saved. Paul writes in 1 Corinthians 15:1-4:

> Now brothers, I want to clarify for you the gospel I proclaimed to you; you received it and have taken your stand on it. You are also saved by it, if you hold to the message I proclaimed to you — unless you believed for no purpose. For I passed on to you as most important what I also received: that Christ died for our sins according to the Scriptures, that He was buried, that He was raised on the third day according to the Scriptures ....

These Scriptures make clear that believing certain facts about Jesus is necessary to be saved. Faith, then, is faith in the truth of facts about Jesus, his birth, death for our sins, and resurrection. But is there more to faith than just believing certain things? Yes, as we're about to see.

# Questions to consider

1. According to John 3:16, what is necessary for eternal life?

2. What did Thomas want to see from Jesus?

3. How many resurrection appearances are there in the New Testament?

4. Which one of Gary Habermas' "minimal facts arguments" do you think is the strongest for proving that Jesus was raised from the dead?

# Truths to remember

1. Whoever believes in Jesus will not perish but have everlasting life.

2. The resurrection of Jesus is not only taught in the New Testament; it's recorded in outside sources, so we can believe this event is true in history.

3. Paul says what we need to believe is of first importance: "Christ died for our sins according to the Scriptures, that He was buried, that He was raised on the third day according to the Scriptures ...."

# PART 5.2 | Faith Is Trusting

MEMORY VERSE - JAS. 2:19
"You believe that God is one; you do well. The demons also believe — and they shudder!"

## Trust

"Wow," you may be thinking, "the demons believe in God?" Yes, they do! The Greek word used here for believing is also the word for faith, *pisteuo*. Are the demons saved from God's judgment because they believe in the death, burial, and resurrection of Jesus? They are not.

You see, faith is more than just believing a certain list of propositions. Faith includes believing a list of things related to the gospel, but saving faith also includes trust. While demons believe the truths contained in the gospel, they don't trust in the gospel to rescue them.

When someone truly believes another person, there is trust in that person. Believing God is expressing trust in him by obedient action. There are many saints in the Scriptures who demonstrate their incredible trust in what God has said. Over the next couple of devotions, we will concentrate on two of them. The first is Noah.

## Things not yet seen

When God gave the command for Noah to build an ark, Noah may have thought he was losing his mind. After all, before this command, no one had seen water fall from the skies. According to Scripture, the first time rain fell was in the great flood (Gen. 7:4, 12). Before this cataclysmic event, water only came from ground sources (Gen. 2:5, 6, 10).

Imagine the mocking that must have come to Noah as he built the ark. This was no quick building project. No one is exactly sure how long the building took, but most likely it was around a hundred years. Imagine those around Noah as he explained what he was doing. They must have thought he had lost his mind, yet Noah trusted God. For an entire century, he trusted God, even though he had never seen rain before.

Hebrews 11:7 says, "By faith Noah, after he was warned about what was not yet seen and motivated by godly fear, built an ark to deliver his family. By faith he condemned the world and became an heir of the righteousness that comes by faith." You can see from this story that Noah's faith in God included a deep trust that what God was telling him was true. True faith includes deep trust.

# Do you trust?

You weren't there when Jesus' resurrection happened, were you? You didn't see Jesus multiply the fish and the loaves and feed the multitudes. How do you know heaven is real? After all, you haven't been there.

We trust these things are true, not only because of the impact Christ had on the world, but because of the trust we have in Christ. Jesus gives us the gift of faith. Of course, we have great reasons to believe everything in the New Testament about Jesus' death, burial, and resurrection, but at the end of the day, you and I weren't actually there to see it.

I trust in Jesus for a lot of reasons. One reason is the accuracy of the New Testament. No other work in history has been transcribed and handed down with such accuracy and clarity as the Bible. I also trust because those who saw Jesus alive again after his resurrection were willing to die for their belief that he actually came back from the dead. All the disciples except John were killed for their faith. Men don't die for a lie.

But finally, I trust because I have experienced the power of Christ in my own life – his love for me, forgiveness, and the gift of repentance. I didn't witness the resurrection of Jesus, but I trust that it's true because of the reasons listed above. Have you trusted in Jesus?

# Questions to consider

1. How can the demons believe, yet not have saving faith?

2. How did Noah prove that he trusted God?

3. What are some proofs in your walk with Christ that you are trusting in him?

# Truths to remember

1. Believing propositional truth about Christ is not the same as a saving faith in Christ.

2. Trusting in Christ is more than believing historical truths. It's experiencing the saving power of God.

3. There are many reasons to trust in the accuracy of the New Testament, the resurrection of Jesus, and the power of God.

# Faith Is Obedient

## MEMORY VERSE - HEB. 11:1
"Now faith is the reality of what is hoped for, the proof of what is not seen. For our ancestors won God's approval by it."

# Fides viva

*Fides viva* is Latin for "living faith." True faith is a faith that is alive and active. As you can see in Hebrews 11, true faith obeys God. In his great work, *Faith Alone*, R. C. Sproul writes, "Martin Luther insisted that the faith that justifies is a *fides viva*, a vital and living faith that yields the fruit of works. Justification is by faith alone, but not by a faith that is alone. Saving faith is not a 'lonely' faith, having no works following as a companion."[3]

Faith moves us to obedient activity in the will of God. Do you have this kind of faith in your life? Think about that for a minute. What actions and activities in your life demonstrate that you have a living, active faith in Jesus?

One of the best examples of a living faith in the Bible is the story of Abraham. It's a crazy story about God testing Abraham and challenging him to sacrifice his only son. What would you do? Would you wait around at the campfire until the next morning to see if God was just kidding, or would you start heading to the place of sacrifice? Let's see what Abraham did.

# God tested Abraham

"So Abraham got up early in the morning, saddled his donkey, and took with him two of his young men and his son Isaac. He split wood for a burnt offering and set out to go to the place God had told him about" (Gen. 22:3). Abraham didn't try to find a loophole. He got up early and with his living, active faith, obeyed immediately. Remember that Isaac's birth was anything but normal. He was born to Abraham's wife Sarah when she was ninety years old.

After the miraculous birth of Isaac, Abraham surely believed God could do anything. Think about what Abraham had witnessed. Romans 4:19 says, "He considered his own body to be already dead (since he was about 100 years old) and also considered the deadness of Sarah's womb, without weakening in the faith." When Isaac was conceived, God supernaturally brought Sarah's womb to life. At ninety years of age, she was no longer barren.

# Mount Moriah

Abraham had seen a dead womb come to life. Now, in Genesis 22, he expects to see his dead son come back to life (Heb. 11:19). This takes faith to an entirely new level. As Abraham's testing draws near, Genesis 22:7-9 says:

> Then Isaac spoke to his father Abraham and said, "My father." And he replied, "Here I am, my son." Isaac said, "The fire and the wood are here, but where is the lamb for the burnt offering?" Abraham answered, "God Himself will provide the lamb for the burnt offering, my son." Then the two of them walked on together. When they arrived at the place that God had told him about, Abraham built the altar there and arranged the wood. He bound his son Isaac and placed him on the altar on top of the wood.

The Hebrew word for provide is *moriah*. More than a thousand years later, on this mountain where Abraham and Isaac faced this test, Solomon's temple would be built (2 Chron. 3:1). Lots of lambs would be slaughtered for the sins of the nation on Mount Moriah. Would Isaac be the first?

Verse 10 of Genesis 22 says, "Then Abraham reached out and took the knife to slaughter his son." In that very moment, the Bible tells us the Lord stopped Abraham. The test was complete. Abraham passed a most difficult examination of faith. He was willing to sacrifice his only son. Verse 13 says, "Abraham looked up and saw a ram caught in the thicket by its horns. So Abraham went and took the ram and offered it as a burnt offering in place of his son."

God provided!

# Great faith

This story is incredible, isn't it? I'm not sure, outside of Jesus following the Father's will to be crucified, that we see a more powerful story of active, living faith. Abraham was willing to take the life of his own son to be obedient to God. I'm guessing that the Lord won't test any of us in that way, but we all have times of testing. Can those around you see that your faith is living and active?

There is an old hymn that says:
> Trust and obey,
> for there's no other way
> to be happy in Jesus,
> but to trust and obey.

Are you believing? Are you trusting? Are you obeying? There's no other way to be happy in Jesus, but to trust and obey.

---

# Questions to consider

1. Do you think you could be as obedient as Abraham?

2. What does *fides viva* mean?

3. Does it amaze you that, after the command to sacrifice his son, Abraham rose early in the morning to obey?

# Truths to remember

1. A living faith is an active faith. Faith moves into the commands of God and is obedient to his call on our lives.

2. The Hebrew word for "provide" is *moriah*. This is a fitting name for the mountain on which God provided for Abraham.

3. God calls us to obey, even when we can't see how God will carry out his plan through us.

# PART 5.4 | Faith Is Personal

### MEMORY VERSE - MATT. 6:6

"But when you pray, go into your private room, shut your door, and pray to your Father who is in secret. And your Father who sees in secret will reward you."

As a college freshman on a football scholarship, I (Brad) was expected to do certain things pertaining to practice, training, diet, and exercise. I knew I was on scholarship, so the funding of my education depended on my practicing and playing well.

One day, I was invited to the Baptist Student Union for lunch. While there, I was intrigued by the fellowship and the message. I began attending regularly, and then I began participating in other BSU events.

About midway through the spring semester, I was told about a summer mission opportunity. The opportunity to serve on mission sounded amazing to me, but there was one problem: football. I had to train during the summer. I had drills to do and practice during the summer.

Football was important because I needed my scholarship. I really felt God's call to go on the mission trip, but I also needed to go to college. What was I going to do? I began to pray about the decision. I asked those I respected for their opinions. Then, I was accepted to go to Alaska for the summer and had to make the decision whether to take the trip. Would I go on mission and forfeit the future I had planned?

This was a decision I had to make myself; no one could make it for me. Others prayed for me and even influenced me, but in the end, the decision was personal. I took the trip, and from that mission trip, God reordered by entire future. The personal decision to follow Jesus allowed me to be where I am today. Faith in Jesus is a personal, individual decision. As you will see, faith is also a growing gift.

# My faith

Just as I had to make a personal decision about the mission trip to Alaska, you must make a personal decision about surrendering your life to Christ and following him each day. Speaking of the individual nature of faith, Paul writes in Galatians 2:20, "... and I no longer live, but Christ lives in me. The life I now live in the body, I live by faith in the Son of God, who loved me and gave Himself for me."

If you look closely, you can see the individual nature of Paul's faith. Paul is saying it is not by his own power that he lives, but by the power of Christ living through him. How did Christ come to live in Paul? Paul has life, and he lives because of his faith in Jesus.

All faith is individual and personal. You will be faced with many choices. There will be many opportunities to sin – to follow your own desires or allow the culture to dictate your life. In each case, you'll have to make a choice to place your faith in God and his Word, or to lay aside what you know to be true and give in to the pressures around you. By trusting in God and placing your faith in Jesus, you have the power to overcome the world. I encourage you to place your faith in Jesus above all things.

# Can it grow?

There's an interesting story in the ninth chapter of Mark's Gospel. Jesus and his disciples are going through a town, and some people come to Jesus and tell him the disciples are unable to cast out a certain demon from a young boy. Jesus asks the boy's father some questions, and the father responds by asking Jesus to help: "But if You can do anything, have compassion on us and help us" (v. 22).

Jesus replies, "'If You can'? Everything is possible to the one who believes" (v. 23). The man gives one of the most honest responses in all the Bible when he says, "I do believe! Help my unbelief" (v. 24).

What's so amazing about this conversation is that the Bible shows us faith is dynamic, not static. Faith can grow and mature. You don't have to stay at the same level of faith for twenty years. This man tells Jesus he has faith, he does believe, but he asks Jesus to help him where his faith is not strong enough.

There's something beautiful and wonderful about the fact that the faith you possess can grow and get stronger. Right now, it may seem as if you have a small faith, but I want to encourage you to press into Jesus and ask him to strengthen your faith. And you know what Jesus will do for you? He will answer that prayer, just like he answered the prayer of that boy's father. Jesus increased the man's faith, and he can and will increase your faith.

Don't be discouraged by a lack of faith or the size of your faith. Ask Jesus to help you believe, and he will.

# Thank you for the gift

Faith is both a gift from God and a response on the part of the individual. This dual nature of faith may seem hard to understand, but the Bible uses two different words to refer to faith. In the Bible, faith is both a noun and verb. How is this possible?

Well, no person is able to have faith on his own because our sin prevents it. Paul shows this when he says, "For you are saved by grace through faith, and this is not from yourselves; it is God's gift — not from works, so that no one can boast" (Eph. 2:8-9).

God, being rich in mercy, through the gospel of Jesus, calls people to himself through faith. He gives the gift of faith to everyone who believes in Jesus. But wait, didn't we say faith was both a gift (noun) and a response (verb)? Paul shows the response of faith when he uses another word for faith: "believe."

Ephesians 1:13 says, "When you heard the message of truth, the gospel of your salvation, and when you believed in Him, you were also sealed with the promised Holy Spirit." God gives the gift of faith, and our response is to receive that faith by believing in the gospel of Jesus for the forgiveness of our sins. While we must choose to respond to God in faith, we thank him for the gift of faith, because he offered us first what we could not do on our own.

# Questions to consider

1. Why is it important that faith in Jesus is individual?

2. Can someone believe in Jesus for you? Why or why not?

3. In what area of your life do you need faith right now?

4. Read Ephesians 2:1-9. Why must faith first be a gift from God?

# Truths to remember

1. Faith is first a gift from God to us.

2. Biblical faith is meant to grow and mature as we grow in Christ.

3. Each person must make a choice to follow Christ; no person can make that decision for another person.

# PART 5.5 | Faith Is Securing

## MEMORY VERSE - HEB. 11:1

"Now faith is the reality of what is hoped for, the proof of what is not seen. For our ancestors won God's approval by it."

# Faith secures justification

A few years ago, my wife and I (Brad) decided to go on a cruise for our tenth anniversary. We picked out the ship, the destination, and the time we wanted to travel. To secure our spots while we made final preparations, we had to give the cruise company a deposit. The deposit not only secured our places on the ship, but also ensured that we were able to fully enjoy all the wonderful amenities of the ship and fun excursions at the destinations. The deposit secured everything that followed.

In addition to the truths about faith you have already learned, faith also has a securing quality about it. For people who place their faith in Christ, faith secures salvation, which includes justification, sanctification, and glorification. I know these are big concepts, but we will unpack them together below.

Justification is an act of God declaring the believing sinner to be in right standing with God. It's like a judge acquitting a person of all charges. This is what God does for us when we trust in Jesus: he says "not guilty" because Christ became guilty in our place, and Christ's righteousness is applied to us.

We discussed repentance and salvation earlier. You learned what it means to repent, and the blessings we receive from repentance. Through the death of Jesus, God makes salvation available to the world. But just because salvation is available to all does not mean everyone in the world is saved. That idea is known as universalism, and it's not biblical. You also learned faith itself is a gift from God, but it also must be applied by each individual person.

Think of it this way: Jesus' death made salvation available to all, but salvation is only applied to those who place their faith in his atoning death. Faith secures salvation. God gives the gift of salvation to the world and the gift of faith through the Holy Spirit. To receive that gift, or to open that gift, each person responds in faith, thus securing the gift as his or her own.

When you place your faith in Jesus, your salvation is secured. The word "secured" is a neat word that means "locked down and safe."

Because your salvation does not depend on you, but on Jesus, your salvation is not subject to the dangers of this world. Jesus says that all those who are in him are secure, and nothing in this world can take them out of his hand (John 10:28-30). This truth is reassuring and brings peace to all who are in Christ.

Because your salvation is secure, you cannot do anything to lose it. There are no mistakes you can commit to make God take back your salvation. Faith has secured salvation for you, and Jesus holds you securely in his own hands.

# Faith secures sanctification

Faith secures your justification. Faith also secures your sanctification. "Sanctification" is a big word that indicates a process through which people become more like Jesus. Sanctification is different from justification. Justification is an act that is complete at a moment in time. Sanctification is a process that continues throughout the life of a Christian. Justification secures you in Jesus, and sanctification makes you more like Jesus. Just as faith brings you into a relationship with Christ, faith also brings you closer to Christ.

Faith, for a Christian, is dynamic. Faith moves and grows. Faith matures over time. Faith helps us understand the depths of Christ's love and reach the heights of his grace. As your faith in Jesus grows, you grow. By faith, you put away the deeds of darkness and put on Jesus (Rom. 13:11-12). By faith you learn to shed your sinful thoughts, words, and actions, and grow in the newness of Jesus (Eph. 4:20-22).

Sanctification is a process that lasts as long as you're alive. The more time you spend with Jesus, reading your Bible and praying, the more your faith in Christ grows, and the more you understand his love for you. This understanding of Christ's love causes you to grow in Christ so that your life has a greater impact for him. As your faith in Jesus grows, you look more like Jesus than you did when you first believed.

# Faith secures glorification

You have learned that faith in Jesus' death, burial, and resurrection secures your justification, and this same faith secures your sanctification. Faith in Jesus also secures your glorification. Paul tells us in Romans 8:30, "And those He predestined, He also called; and those He called, He also justified; and those He justified, He also glorified." What does Paul mean when he says "glorified"?

If sanctification is the process of being made into the image of Jesus, glorification is the completion of that process. Glorification happens when we get to heaven. When Christ returns and brings human history to its glorious end, all those who have placed their faith in Christ will be made perfect and complete, lacking nothing (Jas. 1:4).

The Christian life is bookended by acts, with a process in the middle. Justification is an act in which, by faith in Jesus, our relationship with God is secured. Sanctification is a process that takes place throughout the lives of Christians, in which, by faith, they take on more of the character of Jesus. Because of that faith, at the end of our lives, Christians are glorified, made perfect in Christ.

The act of glorification is beautiful because it removes all the stains of sin from each believer. In heaven, there is no sorrow, grief, or pain. There are no late homework assignments, no bullies, and no teams for which we try out. In heaven, all is made right because all believers are there and experience the fullness of living with one another without the pain of sin. Through faith in Christ, your glorification is secured.

# Questions to consider

1. How does faith in Jesus secure salvation?

2. Is faith something you have on your own?

3. How can your faith grow throughout your life?

4. Why is it important for your faith to grow?

# Truths to remember

1. Jesus secures your salvation, and faith in Jesus applies that work of salvation to you.

2. Your faith in Christ can grow and impact your life for God's glory.

3. Your initial faith in Jesus secures your justification, sanctification, and glorification.

# Memory Verses

**FAITH IS BELIEVING:** "For God loved the world in this way: He gave His One and Only Son, so that everyone who believes in Him will not perish but have eternal life" (John 3:16).

**FAITH IS TRUSTING:** "You believe that God is one; you do well. The demons also believe — and they shudder!" (Jas. 2:19).

**FAITH IS OBEDIENT:** "Now faith is the reality of what is hoped for, the proof of what is not seen. For our ancestors won God's approval by it" (Heb. 11:1).

**FAITH IS PERSONAL:** "But when you pray, go into your private room, shut your door, and pray to your Father who is in secret. And your Father who sees in secret will reward you" (Matt. 6:6).

**FAITH IS SECURING:** "Now faith is the reality of what is hoped for, the proof of what is not seen. For our ancestors won God's approval by it" (Heb. 11:1).

# PART 6 | What Is Prayer?

By Brad Delaughter

Although he has been gone many years now, my Pawpaw (I'm from Mississippi, so we say "Pawpaw") Raymond was the person God used to impact me the most for Christ. Pawpaw was a Christian man with integrity and dignity. He was not boastful or flashy. He was a simple, southern Mississippi man who lived a humble life.

Pawpaw was the person I could talk to about anything. When I was upset, I would go to him and tell him about my struggles. When I was sad as a kid, I could crawl up in his lap and not say a word, and he would just hold me until I felt better. When I was worried, I would express my anxieties to him, and he would listen intently. When I was happy, I would share my victories, and he would rejoice with me.

I learned over my life that, no matter my situation, I could always go to Pawpaw, and with empathy, grace, love, and sometimes sternness, he would listen and bring peace to my heart. When I think of prayer, I think of talking with Pawpaw.

We often think talking to God is difficult and scary. We think we should only "bother" him with the big issues of life. But that's not the God of the Bible. That's not the God who has rescued us in Jesus. God wants to rejoice with us, comfort us, cry with us, and, when needed, correct us. He does all this in love and with a great desire to see us transformed into the image of Jesus.

Prayer and regular Bible intake are the most important aspects of our Christian life. If we think of the Bible as the engine that drives us to Jesus, prayer is the fuel that powers the Word of God in our hearts. Sometimes we think of prayer as complex, but Jesus showed us, in Matthew 6:9-13, that prayer is a simple conversation with our heavenly Father.

Notice how Jesus begins the prayer in verse 9: "Our Father in heaven, Your name be honored as holy." God is our heavenly Father, and, as such, he desires our very best. He is always ready with a listening ear and an open heart to guide us through life.

In this part of our study, we review five aspects of prayer. We see how God desires prayer from us. We also learn how prayer is a partnership between the triune God and us. We discover the simple nature of prayer. We also see that prayer is a continual conversation between God and us.

Finally, we understand the vital nature of prayer in the life of a growing Christian. It is my prayer that, as you read through these chapters, you are strengthened and encouraged in your own prayer life.

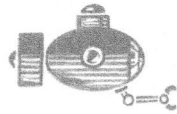

# PART 6.1 | Prayer Is Desired

**MEMORY VERSE - 1 JOHN 5:14**
"Now this is the confidence we have before Him: Whenever we ask anything according to His will, He hears us."

## Prayer brings us near to God

I remember when my wife and I began dating in high school. While my parents loved my future wife, they did not appreciate the fact that I spent several hours a night on the phone with her. Even though I had breakfast and lunch with her every day at school, after I got home from football practice, I would eat dinner, shower, and then my brother and I would fight over the phone, so one of us could be the first to make a call (no iPhones back then!). I would spend time on the phone with her, talking about everything and nothing at all.

Why would I spend so much time talking with her? Because I desired to talk to her. I desired to spend time with her. Even now, after being together more than twenty-two years, and married for seventeen years, we still have a strong desire to talk to each other.

What do we talk about after all these years? Anything and everything. Just like twenty years ago, we tell each other about our day. We laugh at the silly things that happen with each other and our kids. We rejoice at each other's successes, and we are each sad when the other is sad. Then, the next day, we do it again. Why? Because we have a desire to talk to each other.

As much as my wife and I enjoy talking with each other, our heavenly Father enjoys hearing from us even more. I truly believe if we could see how much God wants to talk with us in prayer, it would cause us to increase our prayer life.

Imagine this great truth: The God of the universe, the one who created everything, really does want to hear from you. And he does not just want to hear from you every now and then; he wants to hear from you every day, multiple times a day. There is nothing going on in your life that God does not want to hear about (even though he knows all things).

Psalm 145:18 is a foundational verse in understanding God's desire to hear from us through prayer. This verse says, "The LORD is near all who call out to Him, all who call out to Him with integrity." Look at what the author is telling us about God. When we call upon God, he comes near to us. Why would he do this? Because he desires to be near us, and prayer is a way for God to be near us. God has at least three desires when it comes to hearing about our lives.

# God desires to hear our needs

Growing up in the world today is different than at any previous time in history. While technological achievements have allowed us to prosper in some amazing ways, they also have brought us many challenges. The pressure for perfection in academics, combined with the intense pull to fit in with your friends or peer group, is cause for anxiety. Pressure seems to be coming from all sides, and it may seem as if you're going to boil over with worry.

I want you to know something: God knows what's going on. And what's even more important, God cares about what's going on in your life. He wants to hear from you and help you through this time.

Paul wrote to churches facing a lot of troubles. He told the church in Philippi, "Don't worry about anything, but in everything, through prayer and petition with thanksgiving, let your requests be made known to God. And the peace of God, which surpasses every thought, will guard your hearts and minds in Christ Jesus" (Phil. 4:6-7).

This verse is huge when it comes to our prayer life. God is telling us there is nothing in this world that should cause us extended periods of anxiety. "Anxiety" is another word for worry. Why shouldn't you worry? Because God wants to hear your needs and bring you peace.

Look at how the verses above flow. When you're worried, you can go to God in prayer and tell him why you're worried. You can thank him for the things that are going well in your life (you're alive, loved by God, and saved by Jesus). And then something amazing happens.

As you tell God what's on your heart – your deepest worries – and as you thank him for his blessings in your life, he brings peace to your heart. This peace is no regular peace. The peace God brings to your life is a peace that cannot be fully understood. God's peace guards and protects your heart and your mind. So, don't be afraid to tell God what's bothering you. He wants to know, and he wants to give you peace.

# God desires to hear our confession of sins

You learned earlier about the importance of confession and repentance. But did you understand the wonderful truth about them? God desires to hear the confession of your sins. He wants you to learn confession and true biblical repentance.

I want to show you this with two verses, one from the Old Testament and one from the New Testament. In Psalm 66:19, we learn, "However, God has listened; He has paid attention to the sound of my prayer." In the New Testament, 1 John 1:9 teaches us, "If we confess our sins, He is faithful and righteous to forgive us our sins and to cleanse us from all unrighteousness."

By combining these two verses, what do we learn? God wants to hear your voice. When you go to him in prayer, he actively listens. This is true even when you sin. God has open ears and an open heart for you to bring your sins and shortcomings to him. What's even more amazing is that the second verse has a promise with it. When you come to God and confess your sin to him, he promises to hear you and forgive you.

This is so important to understand. You may think you have "out-sinned" God's ability to forgive you, but that's not true. You can't "out-sin" God's love and grace for you (Rom. 5:20-21). So, no matter how you may feel, whether it's embarrassment or shame from your sin, run to God. He wants to hear from you. And, more importantly, he wants to forgive you and cleanse you.

# God desires to hear our victories

You may imagine that God does not like it when Christians get happy and loud. You might think, "God wants us to enjoy life, but too much joy is not good." This thinking is not biblical. God loves it when Christians enjoy him and his creation. This is good and brings glory to him. Psalm 20:5 tells us, "Let us shout for joy at your victory and lift the banner in the name of our God. May Yahweh fulfill all your requests!"

When God gives you victories in life, two things should happen. You should be joyful, and you should be thankful. Rejoice in what God has given you and thank him for what he has done.

What are some victories for which you can be thankful? When God strengthens you and you do not give in to temptation, you can thank him for victory over sin. When you have courage to stand up for what's right, you can thank God for helping you be brave. When you help someone else get through a tough spot in life, you can thank God for giving you victory through wisdom and compassion.

When you make a good grade on a test or win a big game, you can thank God for giving you knowledge or skill. When you look back over the past month or year and see that you are closer to Christ now than before, you can thank God for the victory that you are more like Christ and are demonstrating his love to others. God loves it when we turn back and praise him, and he desires to hear about our victories.

# Questions to consider

1. Look at Psalm 145:18. What are some reasons you can call upon the Lord in prayer?

2. How does it feel to know that the God of the universe desires to hear from you?

3. What is a need in your life that you can tell God about right now?

4. What is a victory in your life that you can thank God for right now?

# Truths to remember

1. There is never a time when God does not want to hear from you.

2. When you talk to God, you can be open and honest with him about your needs, worries, sins, and victories.

# PART 6.2 | Prayer Is Partnership

MEMORY VERSE - PS. 18:6
"I called to the LORD in my distress, and I cried to my God for help. From His temple He heard my voice, and my cry to Him reached His ears."

## Partnership helps us reach our goals

When I was a kid, my dad worked at a sawmill. We lived in front of the sawmill. Our small front yard was all gravel, located near the highway. The front yard had two tall, skinny pine trees, with the lowest branches a good ten feet off the ground.

My brother, Randy, and I wanted to make a treehouse one weekend. We didn't really know how, but knew we at least needed some wood. We went to the sawmill's lumber yard and "borrowed" a few twelve-foot boards.

I painfully shimmied up one of the pine trees. Once I reached the first limb, Randy began pushing boards to me, and I pulled them up and laid them across to the adjacent tree. We worked back and forth, raising and lowering the boards, hammer, and nails until we had all three pieces connected to both trees. We did it! We had our tree house.

While this story is silly, I tell it to illustrate an important point. My brother and I had to work in partnership to achieve our goal. I put in some work, and he put in some work. We helped each other. You may not think so, but prayer also is a partnership. Prayer is a partnership with God, with others, and with your church.

## Partnership with God

It may seem strange to think of prayer as a partnership with God, but that is exactly the nature of prayer. When you pray, you're connecting to the God of the universe, the maker of heaven and earth. You're lifting your mind, heart, and voice to the very one who made you. God cares deeply for you, and, like your parents, he desires to connect with you.

One of the ways we connect with God is through prayer. We will look at several Bible verses to help us see this great truth. The first part of James 4:8 tells us, "Draw near to God, and He will draw near to you." It's great to know that when you come close to God, he comes closer to you. Even though you may have sinned or disobeyed his Word, when you come to God honestly and sincerely, the Bible says God draws near to you as well.

God also wants to hear your prayers. Just as your parents want to hear what's going on in your life, how it's affecting you, and how you're thinking about your life, God wants to hear from you. Psalm 66:19 says, "However, God has listened; He has paid attention to the sound of my prayer." In this Psalm, the author is letting us know a wonderful truth: God hears us when we pray. God pays attention to his children when we pray. As you talk to God, he not only listens; he enjoys listening to you, no matter what you're praying.

But what happens when you're struggling in life, and you have a hard time praying, or knowing what to pray? Does God just leave you to suffer by yourself? Does he simply wait for you to find the right words to pray before he listens and answers? Thankfully, the Bible tells us this is not the case.

Writing to the church in Rome, Paul says, "In the same way the Spirit also joins to help in our weakness, because we do not know what to pray for as we should, but the Spirit Himself intercedes for us with unspoken groanings" (Rom. 8:26). Now, there is a lot we can unpack in this verse, but I want to highlight one thing: When we go to God in prayer and don't know what to pray, the Holy Spirit prays for us. Isn't it wonderful that God cares enough to not only listen and answer your prayers, but to help you pray when you don't know how?

# Partnership with others

Prayer not only is a partnership with God, but also a partnership with others. When you pray with and for others, it's like you're all on the same side in a tug-of-war contest. Prayer unites believers in both mission and purpose as we talk to God, fight spiritual battles, and pursue God's will.

In Acts 2:42, the church is focused on the words of Jesus, sharing with fellow Christians, taking the Lord's supper, and praying. Notice they were together, partnering with one another. Luke shows us the result in Acts 2:47: "... praising God and having favor with all the people. And every day the Lord added to them those who were being saved."

The Bible also shows us the power of prayer when Peter is arrested for sharing the gospel, and, in Acts 12:7, we learn an angel has released him from prison. Upon his release, he goes to the place where his friends are gathered and finds "many had assembled and were praying" (Acts 12:12). Believers prayed for Peter, and God released him.

Galatians 6:2 says, "Carry one another's burdens; in this way you will fulfill the law of Christ." When you partner with others in prayer, you are helping to bear their burdens. You can pray with someone, and you can pray for someone. In both passages we read from the Book of Acts, believers are praying with others and for others.

Prayer is a powerful way you can partner with others for the gospel. Prayer is a way to let others know you care for them and are sympathetic with their struggles. Prayer is a great way to partner for the sake of the gospel.

# Partnership with the church

It's true that prayer is a partnership with God and others, but prayer also is a partnership with the church of God. When the church partners together in prayer, united in purpose, God does amazing things. Following Jesus' ascension, his followers gathered in an upper room. Luke records that these believers focused on one thing – prayer (Acts 1:14). Their praying together led to the pouring out of the Holy Spirit on the church during Pentecost.

When the church partners in prayer, big things happen. Prayer has preceded the great moves of God throughout the history of the church. The great Welsh revival of 1904-1905 saw thousands of people come to saving faith in Jesus. History shows that this revival. like all true revivals, was preceded by constant and sincere prayer.

Do you want to reach your family, friends, and school for Jesus? Would you like to see others impacted by Christ? Join with your church to pray for a revival and a movement of God in your life, your church, and your community.

## Questions to consider

1. Review the verses on partnership with God. Why is it important to understand prayer as a partnership?

2. How can you develop a better habit of partnering with God in prayer?

3. How do you feel knowing God wants to partner with you and help you in prayer?

4. Who are two people you can pray for right now?

5. Who are two people with whom you can pray in the coming days?

## Truths to remember

1. Prayer is a partnership between you, God, others, and the church.

2. You don't have to have all the right words in prayer. Pray openly and honestly, and trust God to know your heart.

# PART 6.3 | Prayer Is Simple

MEMORY VERSE - JAS. 4:8
"Draw near to God, and He will draw near to you. Cleanse your hands, sinners, and purify your hearts, double-minded people!"

## A simple act of conversation

Sometimes prayer seems so scary because we think it's complex. We overthink prayer, and in doing so, we make difficult what God intends to be a simple act of conversation. In teaching our children to pray, I try to be as simple as possible. When the kids are ready for bed, I ask them a few questions: "Is there anything you can thank God for?" "Is there anybody you can pray for?" "Is there anything you need God to help you with?" "Is there anything you need to tell God you are sorry for?" Then, after answering these questions, we spend about two minutes in prayer.

Can prayers be deeper and more complex than these simple prayers? Sure, but they don't have to be. When walking on the water toward Jesus, Peter took his eyes off Jesus, and as he was sinking, he simply prayed, "Lord, save me" (Matt. 14:30). What was Jesus' response to such a short prayer? Jesus reached out his hand, took hold of Peter, and saved him (v. 31).

During Jesus' life, there was a group of religious people known as the Pharisees. This group loved to impress people by praying long, loud prayers in public. In contrast to the Pharisees' prayers, Jesus provided a model for prayer in Matthew 6 that is only six short sentences. Jesus' prayer shows us just how simple prayer can be for a Christian. Look at Jesus' Model Prayer here:

> Therefore, you should pray like this: Our Father in heaven, Your name be honored as holy. Your kingdom come. Your will be done on earth as it is in heaven. Give us today our daily bread. And forgive us our debts, as we also have forgiven our debtors. And do not bring us into temptation, but deliver us from the evil one. [For Yours is the kingdom and the power and the glory forever. Amen.] (Matt. 6:9-13)

The Model Prayer gives us an example of how to pray. In this prayer, there are elements of praise, repentance, asking, and yielding. You may think prayer can't be that simple, but prayer *is* that simple. Using Jesus' prayer as a model, I want to show you a simple way to learn and practice prayer. The model you will learn is the "P.R.A.Y." model:

**P** PRAISE
Spend time praising God for who he is and what he has done.

**R** REPENT
Confess your sin to God and ask for forgiveness.

**A** ASK
Ask God for what you and others need.

**Y** YIELD
Talk to God about your desire to obey him in your life.

# Praise

Jesus begins the Model Prayer by reminding us that the Father is in heaven and his name is "hallowed" (Matt. 6:9 KJV). This means God's name is above all other names, that God is bigger than anything else, and that he deserves praise, honor, and glory. You can spend time praising God for who he is and what he has done in your life. When you praise God for who he is, you are praising God for his character.

What are some character traits of God you can praise? God is worthy (Luke 19:37-40). God is creator (Col. 1:16). God is Savior (1 Tim. 2:3-4). God is holy (Heb. 7:26). God is righteous (2 Cor. 5:21). God is gracious (Ps. 103:8). God is loving (John 3:16). These are wonderful places to start when praising God for his character.

You can also praise God for what he has done. What has God done in your life? God created you, he has nurtured you, he has saved you in Jesus, and he has given you food to eat, clothes to wear, and a roof under which to sleep. These are simple, but important, things to remember when you praise God.

# Repent

You learned earlier about repentance. Repentance should be a regular part of your prayer life. When we repent, we recognize our sin, confess it to God, and turn from our sin. Jesus shows us the importance of repentance and asking for forgiveness in Matthew 6:12. You can forgive those who have wronged you, because you recognize that, if a holy and righteous God can forgive you, you can forgive others.

# Ask

My wife and I have four children. Kids instinctively know how to ask for things. Sometimes they ask for things they need, such as help learning to tie their shoes. At other times, the requests are based purely on want, such as getting a snack from the store. When it comes to our relationship with God, we can forget how to ask.

You might be nervous to ask God because you don't want to bother him. Or, perhaps, you may think your request is weird. Well, you don't need to worry about either of these. Jesus tells us in Matthew 6:8 that God knows what's on our hearts even before we ask. So, go ahead. Just like my children are never a bother when they come to me, you are never a bother to God when you come to him and ask him to meet your needs, or to satisfy your wants.

# Yield

Part of being a child of God is learning more about him as our heavenly Father. Our Father in heaven knows all, has all wisdom, and possesses all power. This means he knows absolutely what is best for your life, even when you don't. Since you know God loves you unconditionally, and you know he wants the best for you in life, you can yield your life to him with confidence.

To yield means to surrender. You can surrender your life to God's will, and you can learn to submit your will, motivations, thoughts, actions, and words to him. In doing so, you are submitting for the sake of his glory. In prayer, you can wrestle with this truth and ask God to help you yield your life to his will.

# Questions to consider

1. After reading this chapter, how have your thoughts on the simple nature of prayer changed?

2. Of the four parts of a simple prayer, which one seems easiest for you right now? Why?

3. Which part of a simple prayer seems most difficult for you right now? Why?

4. How can you use the P.R.A.Y. model to teach someone else to pray?

# Truths to remember

1. Prayer is simple.

2. You don't have to use a formula to pray. You can pray what is on your heart because God already knows about it.

# PART 6.4 | Prayer Is Continual

**MEMORY VERSES - 1 THESS. 5:16-18**
"Rejoice always! Pray constantly. Give thanks in everything,
for this is God's will for you in Christ Jesus."

## Talking with the one you love

My wife and I have been together since she was a freshman in high school – twenty-two years total – and married for seventeen of those years. There were times I had to work long hours, only to return home after she was already in bed. There were times I had to travel for work and was away for days at a time. There were times we were unable to see each other for various reasons. Throughout these years, we've had to be apart for many reasons, but there was one thing we always did, no matter our physical distance from one another: talk.

We talk to one another all the time. We talk by text, phone, and Facetime. When we're at home or driving in the car, we talk. When we wake up in the morning and go to bed at night, we talk. You may think after more than twenty years, we would run out of things to say.

Why do we talk so much? Because we love each other. And the more we talk, the more we grow in our love for one another. Prayer works that way. The more you talk with God, the more your love for him grows, and the deeper your relationship with him grows.

The Bible tells us prayer is essential to our lives. You've learned the simple nature of prayer. Because prayer is so simple to your life as a Christian, you can make prayer a continual part of your life, every day.

In the memory verse above, Paul is encouraging the Thessalonian church to be a people of prayer. Notice that Paul says "always," "without ceasing," and "in everything." These should be continual actions in your life. There should not be a time when you're not rejoicing, praying, and being thankful. And did you catch the really cool line in verse 18? Paul says these actions are part of God's will for your life as a follower of Jesus.

Rejoicing and thanksgiving are part of a believer's prayer life. Why would God want each believer to pray continually? Prayer is a vital part of the life of a growing, maturing, believer in Christ. As such, prayer is a practice you should establish at the beginning of each day. Prayer is something you can do throughout the day. Prayer is a practice with which you can end your day. From these three verses, we learn three important truths about prayer.

# Established in prayer

When you wake up, you can establish your day with God by beginning with prayer. Since you know you're to rejoice always, you can begin your day by rejoicing. To rejoice means to give thanks. There's not a time in your life when you cannot rejoice.

What can you rejoice about when you wake up? Start by thanking God for giving you a place to sleep, giving you the ability to sleep, and waking you. Next, take a few minutes to practice the P.R.A.Y. model you learned in the previous chapter. By establishing your day in prayer, you're allowing the Holy Spirit to fill your heart and mind, giving you a godly mindset to encounter all God has for you that day.

# Engage in prayer

To pray without ceasing means you never stop. The practices of being happy with God, praying, and being thankful are habits you can develop throughout your life – no matter where you are, no matter what you're doing, and no matter your circumstances. This is good news.

You can engage in prayer when you're about to take a big test. You can engage in prayer when you receive a good grade on that test. You can ask God to help you face a difficult conversation with a friend. You can ask God to help you with tryouts for the team. You can rejoice in Jesus when a friend comes to faith in Christ. And you can ask for courage to share Christ with a classmate.

You can ask in prayer for safety when you're driving somewhere. You can ask for wisdom about how to handle a relationship. God wants to give you wisdom and strength in every area of your life. Praying throughout the day gives you direct access to the throne room of God, allowing you to receive the fullness of his power.

# End in prayer

In Psalm 55:17, the psalmist declares, "I complain and groan morning, noon, and night, and He hears my voice." The author is in constant prayer at this time of his life. He's in a difficult place, and he's going to the Lord in the morning, throughout the day, and when he goes to sleep. Why does he do this? Psalm 121:4 provides the answer: "Indeed, the Protector of Israel does not slumber or sleep."

God does not have a bedtime, and he does not sleep. Just as you start your day with prayer and pray throughout the day, you can also finish your day with prayer. As you lie down, review your day. Thank God for the good things. Celebrate the wins. Repent of sins and bad decisions. Trust in his forgiveness. Ask God to give you a good night's sleep. Then, with the full assurance of God's love for you, go to sleep. And when you wake, you can begin the wonderful process of establishing your day with prayer again.

# Questions to consider

1. What are some specific needs or wants you can pray for throughout the day?

2. What are two blessings you can thank God for right now?

3. Why is it important to start and end your day with prayer?

# Truths to remember

1. Begin your day with prayer and end your day with prayer.

2. Prayer can be used at any time throughout your day.

# PART 6.5 | Prayer Is Vital

**MEMORY VERSE - MATT. 6:6**
"But when you pray, go into your private room, shut your door, and pray to your Father who is in secret. And your Father who sees in secret will reward you."

## Vital to our spiritual lives

When I was a teenager, I was driving home one night during a terrible thunderstorm. I was going down a hill into a curve that led to an old wooden bridge with no guard rails. As I went down the hill, the wet, loose gravel caught my tires and sent me spinning onto the bridge. When my truck stopped, half was hanging off the bridge, with only the back wheels barely on the bridge. The truck was teetering on the edge. I needed that bridge. It was the only thing that kept me from plunging into the water below. The bridge was vital to my life that night.

What we've discussed in this part of our study leads us to this point: Prayer is vital for the Christian life. God desires our prayers. Prayer is an intimate partnership between God and believers. Prayer is simple. Prayer is continual. This leads to the natural conclusion that prayer is vital.

Christian apologist C. S. Lewis once said, "I pray because I can't help myself. I pray because the need flows out of me all the time, waking and sleeping. It doesn't change God. It changes me."[1] Why would Lewis make this statement? Because prayer is vital for the follower of Jesus.

In Matthew 6:5-8, Jesus provides instruction on prayer:

> Whenever you pray, you must not be like the hypocrites, because they love to pray standing in the synagogues and on the street corners to be seen by people. I assure you: They've got their reward! But when you pray, go into your private room, shut your door, and pray to your Father who is in secret. And

your Father who sees in secret will reward you. When you pray, don't babble like the idolaters, since they imagine they'll be heard for their many words. Don't be like them, because your Father knows the things you need before you ask Him.

While there are several things going on in this passage, I want to focus on the first word Jesus says: "When." Jesus is assuming that believers pray. Jesus does not say "if" you pray, but "when" you pray. Why does Jesus expect his followers to pray? Because prayer is vital to the life of a follower of Jesus. Jesus himself prayed to the Father, so why would his followers not pray? There are several reasons prayer is vital for the follower of Jesus.

## Prayer keeps you connected to God

You learned in the previous chapter that prayer can establish your day. You also learned that you can pray throughout the day, as well as end your day with prayer. By utilizing prayer from the time you wake up until you go to sleep, you stay connected with God throughout the day.

The Gospel accounts show Jesus praying more than thirty times. These passages display the continual nature of Jesus' prayer life. Why did Jesus pray so much? Jesus, like us, needed to be connected to the Father through prayer. Prayer connects you to God and his power for your life.

The Christian life is one of power through the Holy Spirit. When you're engaged in continual prayer, you stay connected to God. Just as you want to converse regularly with those close to you, prayer connects you with and keeps you close to God.

## Prayer reminds you that you're part of something bigger

When you're connected to God through prayer on a regular basis, you soon realize you're part of something much bigger than you can imagine. You learned earlier that prayer connects you to God and is a partnership between you and God. Prayer also joins you with all followers of Jesus. When you pray, you can expand your reach across the world.

When Paul instructed the Ephesian Christians in prayer, he showed them the impact of their prayers: "Pray at all times in the Spirit with every prayer and request, and stay alert in this with all perseverance and intercession for all the saints" (Eph. 6:18). Notice Paul's words. He encourages the Ephesians to continue in prayer with every request for all the saints. Prayer allows you to partner with believers in unique ways.

Prayer also allows you to engage in spiritual warfare. Just a few verses earlier, Paul shows the spiritual nature of prayer when he says, "For our battle is not against flesh and blood, but against the rulers, against the authorities, against the world powers of this darkness, against the spiritual forces of evil in the heavens" (Eph. 6:12). Prayer reminds you that you're part of a cosmic battle, and when you join forces with other believers in prayer, you're joining the spiritual forces in heaven for the glory of God.

# Prayer makes you more like Jesus

Yes, prayer connects you to God, and prayer reminds you that you're a part of something bigger than yourself. But the most vital reason to make prayer a regular part of your life is that prayer makes you more like Jesus. Continually coming before God and practicing the model of P.R.A.Y. helps you grow in the character of Jesus.

The more you spend time in the Bible, and the more you pray through the Bible, the more you see your need to depend on Jesus. As you spend time meditating on Jesus and thanking Jesus for his goodness, your appreciation for the beauty and wonder of Jesus grows.

As you grow in your prayer life, you begin to take on the character and qualities of Jesus such as humility, gentleness, kindness, compassion, and love. Prayer puts you in the position to learn about Jesus, to submit to Jesus, and to live like Jesus.

Prayer is vital to your life. I encourage you to develop the practice of prayer, because it is the power that fuels your walk with Jesus. Prayer allows your life to have an impact for Jesus in ways you cannot imagine.

Remember, start small with prayer. Prayer is desired by God, it's a partnership, it's simple, it's to be continual, and it's vital for your life as a follower of Jesus.

# Questions to consider

1. Why is being connected to God important for your walk as a follower of Jesus?

2. How do you feel, knowing prayer connects you to a cosmic playing field of spiritual warfare, and knowing your prayers play a part in the outcome?

3. In what ways can prayer help make you more like Jesus?

# Truths to remember

1. Prayer is vital to the health and growth of every follower of Jesus.

2. The more we practice biblical praying, the more like Jesus we become.

# Memory verses

**PRAYER IS DESIRED:** "Now this is the confidence we have before Him: Whenever we ask anything according to His will, He hears us" (1 John 5:14).

**PRAYER IS PARTNERSHIP:** "I called to the LORD in my distress, and I cried to my God for help. From His temple He heard my voice, and my cry to Him reached His ears" (Ps. 18:6).

**PRAYER IS SIMPLE:** "Draw near to God, and He will draw near to you. Cleanse your hands, sinners, and purify your hearts, double-minded people!" (Jas. 4:8).

**PRAYER IS CONTINUAL:** "Rejoice always! Pray constantly. Give thanks in everything, for this is God's will for you in Christ Jesus" (1 Thess. 5:16-18).

**PRAYER IS VITAL:** "But when you pray, go into your private room, shut your door, and pray to your Father who is in secret. And your Father who sees in secret will reward you" (Matt. 6:6).

# PART 7 | What Is Love?

By Daniel Carr

In her 1984 hit song, "What's Love Got to Do with It," Tina Turner answers the song's question by suggesting that love is a mere emotion. Is that all there is to love?

As a culture, we're inundated with ideas of what love is. Romance novels, Hollywood films, and TV series are littered with the message that love is what we fall in or out of. From true love in *The Princess Bride* to the romantic love that conquers barriers and obstacles in *The Notebook*, we are confronted with the message that falling in love with someone is the greatest of all experiences and is the absolute best for which we can hope.

No doubt, meeting someone, falling in love, and getting married is a fantastic experience. However, if falling in love and getting married is so great, then why doesn't everyone get married and stay that way? According to a 2021 Pew Research Center study of 2019 Census Bureau data, only 53 percent of adults ages 25-54 are married.[1]

Additionally, if this is the greatest of all experiences, why are fewer people pursuing it? The 2019 data shows the percentage of married adults fell to 53 percent in 2019 from 67 percent in 1990. Even among those who experience romantic love, 41 percent of first-time marriages end in divorce. Although that means the majority of first marriages endure, two out of five do not. If that's the greatest of all human experiences – if that's all love is – then many of us miss out.

Perhaps another explanation is that we've set our minds and our standards too low. What if love is more than just the romantic bond between husband and wife? What if love is more than a second-hand emotion? In this part, we explore what the Bible teaches about love. Maybe God will expand not only your understanding of love, but your experience of his love.

# PART 7.1 | Three Kinds of Love

## MEMORY VERSES - MATT. 22:37-39

"He said to him, 'Love the Lord your God with all your heart, with all your soul, and with all your mind. This is the greatest and most important command. The second is like it: Love your neighbor as yourself.'"

## One word, three meanings

The other day, a gracious couple invited my wife and me to dinner. "Where would you like to go?" they asked. Our reply was immediate: "Red Lobster!" Our friends responded, "Oh ... you must love seafood." We sure do.

What do we mean by the phrase, "We love seafood"? Does that reference to love carry the same meaning as when I look into my wife's eyes and say, "I love you"? Of course not. But we use the same word.

The New Testament was written in Greek. Unlike English-speaking people, the Greeks employed different words when discussing different concepts that we lump together in the word "love." In New Testament times, three different words were used for love.

## *Eros*

The Greek word *eros* refers to the "passionate, healthy, physical expression of arousal and sexual love between a husband and wife."[2] We get our word "erotic" from this Greek word. Although this word is not used in Scripture, many Scriptures refer to this aspect of love. One example is 1 Corinthians 7:8-9, in which Paul writes: "I say to the unmarried and to widows: It is good for them if they remain as I am. But if they do not have self-control, they should marry, for it is better to marry than to burn with desire."

## Phileo

The Greek word *phileo* means love as in friendship.[3] This word is used to depict personal relationships such as friendships. In fact, the city of Philadelphia literally means "the city of brotherly love." The brotherly love portion of the moniker comes from the first portion of the city's Greek name "Phila," or *phileo*.

This word is used many times in Scripture. For example, Jesus teaches in Matthew 10:37: "The person who loves (*phileo*) father or mother more than Me is not worthy of Me; the person who loves (*phileo*) son or daughter more than Me is not worthy of Me."

## Agape

The New Testament uses *agape* exclusively to "express that spiritual bond of love between God and man and between man and man, in Christ, which is characteristic of Christianity."[4] *Agape* refers to that supernatural and unconditional love God has for his people, as in John 3:16: "For God loved (*agape*) the world in this way: He gave His One and Only Son, so that everyone who believes in Him will not perish but have eternal life."

*Agape* is also the love that believers are to have for one another. Jesus says in Matthew 22:39, "Love (*agape*) your neighbor as yourself."

In Greek, this subtle difference between natural love (*phileo*) and supernatural love (*agape*) is rarely seen. In fact, the two words could serve as synonyms. In John 21, Jesus leverages this subtle difference to teach Peter a lesson he'd never forget.

## Do you love me?

Peter denied Jesus three times in Jesus' most desperate moments. One cannot imagine the guilt and shame Peter felt at having denied his Lord – especially after he had boastfully claimed hours earlier that he was willing to die for Jesus. Now, Jesus has been crucified, buried, and resurrected, and he's making appearances to many of his followers. But Peter is still haunted with shame.

One morning, recounted in John 21, the disciples are fishing and see Jesus on the shore. They rush to him and sit down to eat breakfast with him. During this meal, a powerful and restorative conversation takes place. It is in this conversation that Jesus leverages the subtle difference between *agape* and *phileo:*

> JESUS: "Simon, son of John, do you love (*agape*) Me more than these?"

> PETER: "Yes, Lord," he said to Him, "You know that I love (*phileo*) You."

> JESUS AGAIN: "Simon, son of John, do you love (*agape*) Me?"

> PETER AGAIN: "Yes, Lord, You know that I love (*phileo*) You."

> JESUS, A THIRD TIME: "Simon, son of John, do you love (*phileo*) Me?"

> PETER, NOW GRIEVED: "Lord, You know everything! You know that I love (*phileo*) You" (John 21:15-17).

Did you catch what happened? At first, Peter, in his mind, is merely substituting the synonym *phileo* for Jesus' use of *agape*. The first two times Jesus asks Peter if he "agapes" him, Peter replies that he "phileoes" him. The third time, Jesus downgrades to asking Peter if he "phileoes" him. It was then Peter realizes what Jesus was really asking.

Peter denied Jesus three times because he only loved Jesus with a natural love. It's the only love a fallen man can give. Jesus is teaching Peter that he needs to love Jesus with unconditional, supernatural *agape* love.

Do you love Jesus with *agape* love? No matter what happens, do you continue to worship him and adore him? Or is your love for Jesus only when things are going great – or when you need something?

# Questions to consider

1. How would you explain the difference between *agape* and *phileo*?

2. How has God shown you his *agape* love?

3. What is an experience you've had in which someone only loved you with *phileo,* or conditional, love?

4. Who is someone, other than Jesus, who has loved you with *agape* love?

# Truths to remember

1. God loves you unconditionally with his perfect and supernatural *agape* love.

2. You are called (and even commanded) to love others with that same supernatural *agape* love that comes from the Spirit of God dwelling in believers.

# PART 7.2 | Love Is a Decision

## MEMORY VERSE - 1 JOHN 4:10

"Love consists in this: not that we loved God, but that He loved us and sent His Son to be the propitiation for our sins."

## A father's love

I will never forget the kids' game, Pretty Pretty Princess. One of my older daughters got this game for Christmas one year. At that time in our family's growth, we had two daughters, and my wife was pregnant with our first son. I love my girls. Yet that love would be challenged.

Upon opening their presents, the girls immediately wanted to play Pretty Pretty Princess. This game consisted of a small board with a spinner and several costume jewelry items such as bracelets, necklaces, rings, earrings, and tiaras. The object of the game was to be the first person to get all your jewelry on as you spun the spinner to land on pictures of the various accessories.

Of course, my girls wanted me to play with them. Honestly, the thought of donning earrings and tiaras was repulsive to me. I had no desire. However, I loved my girls who were, at this point, using the ultimate manipulative taunt, "Please, Daddy, please." So, I decided to play Pretty Pretty Princess with them. It would be the first of many rounds of the game we would play through the years. And no, there are no pictures.

## God's love

So often, we learn what the Scriptures have always said – love is so much more than an emotion. Love is demonstrated as a commitment through multiple decisions. God has ultimately demonstrated his love for us through his decision to send Jesus. The Father did not merely have an emotional moment; he faced a gut-wrenching, painful decision. He would send his only Son from heaven and into his creation, which mankind had turned into a pit of sin and debauchery.

There were no warm fuzzies, no watching his Son leave home, knowing he'd be just fine. No, the Father was sending his Son to his certain death – an excruciating and humiliating death. This was the Father loving us through his decision. The Bible says in Romans 5:8, "But God proves His own love for us in that while we were still sinners, Christ died for us!"

What makes this love of God and his decision more profound is that we did not and do not deserve it. Often, we make loving decisions out of a desire to reward or honor someone. We take our kids out to a special dinner when they make good grades, or we celebrate as a team when we win a championship.

Such rewards and gifts are not at play in this scenario of God sending his Son. Romans 5:8 says, "while we were still sinners." God was not rewarding us for our achievements by sending Jesus. We didn't manipulate his decision. We didn't sway him. He simply chose. He simply loved us.

# Jesus' love

In the same way, Jesus loves us unconditionally. As Jesus nears his crucifixion, we see examples of his determination to give himself because of his love. He reminds his disciples in John 15:9, "As the Father has loved Me, I have also loved you. Remain in My love." He also teaches them in John 15:13, "No one has greater love than this, that someone would lay down his life for his friends."

For Jesus, this is not an isolated decision, but a moment-by-moment decision to proceed toward his death. At his arrest, dozens of soldiers show up, armed and ready to arrest Jesus and his disciples. Peter, in a typical brash response, draws his sword and is ready for action. Jesus makes a revealing comment to Peter in that moment:

> Put your sword back in its place because all who take up a sword will perish by a sword. Or do you think that I cannot call

on My Father, and He will provide Me at once with more than 12 legions of angels? How, then, would the Scriptures be fulfilled that say it must happen this way? (Matt. 26:52-54).

John also records Jesus saying in this same conversation, "Am I not to drink the cup the Father has given Me?" (John 18:11).

These startling rhetorical questions reveal Jesus making a decision, moment by moment, to continue his journey to the cross. He did this because of his love for the Father. Because he loved the Father, Jesus wanted to obey his Father's will, even if it meant enduring the most horrific death imaginable – death by crucifixion. His love moved him to decide, moment by moment, to honor the Father.

Jesus also made these moment-by-moment decisions because of his *agape* love for us. The author of Hebrews even refers to Jesus' honoring the Father, and saving us, as his joy. He writes, "... keeping our eyes on Jesus, the source and perfecter of our faith, who for the joy that lay before Him endured a cross and despised the shame and has sat down at the right hand of God's throne" (Heb. 12:2).

Jesus could have stopped at any time. He had that right and authority. As he told Peter, he could have summoned twelve legions (72,000) of angels to deliver him. Yet, moment by moment, Jesus continued his brutal journey of love. His love is constant. There has never been a time when Jesus has loved you any more than he does right now.

I recently counseled a couple whose marriage seemed to be falling apart. The husband confessed to having been unfaithful to his wife with another woman. This wasn't a one-time event, but an ongoing affair that lasted months. The wife was crushed, betrayed, ashamed, and wanted nothing to do with the husband anymore. She wanted a divorce – and she had that right.

As we met, read Scripture, and prayed, the Lord said to her heart that he wanted her to choose to keep loving her husband and forgive him. She wrestled with this for weeks, as she did not want the marriage to continue. Every time she looked at her husband, she was reminded of her embarrassment and his betrayal. Then, at one of our sessions, she made her decision. She told her husband that she was choosing to love him. She was willing to work towards forgiveness and reconciliation. She likely did not feel as if she loved him, but she chose to love him.

Like Jesus, we are to choose, moment by moment, to love God and each other. We won't always feel like doing this. But *agape* love is unconditional, steadfast, and constant. Do you love that way?

# Questions to consider

1. When was a time you had to choose to love someone, even when you did not feel like it?

2. Do you look at yourself as someone Jesus should love or someone who truly does not deserve his love? Why?

3. How do you still love someone who has betrayed you?

# Truths to remember

1. Jesus chose to die for us because he loves the Father and wanted nothing more than to obey his will.

2. Jesus chose to die for us, not because we earned it, but because he loves us.

3. There has never been a time when Jesus has loved you any more than he does right now.

# PART 7.3 | Love Is a Christian's Trademark

**MEMORY VERSE - JOHN 13:35**
"By this all people will know that you are My disciples,
if you have love for one another."

## Godly love makes all the difference

There once was a young girl growing up in a highly dysfunctional home. Her father was an alcoholic and womanizer; her mom tried to hold things together the best she could. The girl's parents would fight regularly, sometimes physically. She was the oldest of three girls, and this young girl felt like she was being tossed around in a storm. Her mom believed in Jesus and knew she should be taking her girls to church – even without her husband. But it was so hard when the father of the family didn't lead spiritually.

Finally, the mother got her girls to Vacation Bible School. During the week, the mom and girls met people who loved them. They prayed for them, gave them some food each day, and – most importantly – shared the gospel with them. The girl and her younger sister both trusted in Christ that week. She would never forget how loved she felt. That love changed her life.

The family soon moved to a new state and, because of the ongoing battles between Mom and Dad, did not go to church. Then this young girl – a teenager by this point – discovered a group of people that drove a church van into her neighborhood every Sunday morning to pick up those who wanted to go to church. The teenage girl got on board and went to the church that sent the van. Once again, she met a group of people who loved her, prayed for her, and encouraged her – just like when she was younger.

By this time, her parents were divorcing. Her mom had finally had enough of the drunkenness, abuse, and adultery. With all this going on, plus trying to provide for her three girls by herself, her mom had little time to spend with her teenage daughter. But the people in the church stepped up to love her.

The gospel, and the love of God through his people at two churches, forever changed the life of that teenage girl. She's a strong follower of Jesus to this day and is married to a pastor – me. *Agape* love in action makes all the difference in the world.

# Love – the true test

We've already discussed how *agape* love is demonstrated through obedience and decisions. Hopefully, you're seeing that love is much more than a mere emotion or comfort zone. Love manifests itself through sacrifice, compassion, service, forgiveness, obedience, and affection.

In the memory verse for this chapter, Jesus teaches his disciples that people will know his followers by how well they love. When the world sees the sacrifice, compassion, obedience, commitment, and service of Christ's disciples, they see love in action – and God is love.

John writes, "The one who does not love does not know God, because God is love" (1 John 4:8). Since God is love, Christians are to live out that love, because the Spirit of God lives within all believers. Christians are different. True Christians are recognized by their actions of love.

Many Christians judge their maturity in Christ by other factors: Do you live a moral life? Do you know a lot about the Bible? Can you quote many Scriptures? Do you go to church? Even though these factors can reflect godly qualities, they're not the true test of whether we are followers of Jesus. Jesus says the true test – the solid evidence that someone is his follower – is his or her love.

Sadly, the church, throughout its history, has had dark seasons when there was not much love demonstrated. Often, as the non-Christian world looks at the church today, it doesn't see love; it sees division and pride.

What if the world saw our love in action much more often? What if our love for Christ and his gospel compelled ALL his church to invade this world with his love?

When we live out God's love in us, we're doing God's good works. Jesus says this in Matthew 5:16: "In the same way, let your light shine before men, so that they may see your good works and give glory to your Father in heaven."

God's love is so powerful. His love in us is powerful. His love, shown by those two churches, eternally changed the trajectory of my wife's life. If someone observed your life for a week, would they see evidence of love that would move them to conclude you really follow Jesus?

## Questions to consider

1. Who has loved you in a way that forever changed your life? If that person is still alive, send him or her a message, or call and say, "Thank you."

2. Who have you loved with God's love so that it made a big impact in their lives?

3. How do you measure your maturity in Christ?

## Truths to remember

1. How we love is the true evidence of whether we're genuine followers of Jesus.

2. A true Christian is compelled by God's love to deliver the gospel.

# PART 7.4 | Love Is Supernatural

## The love test

How loving a person are you? Let's try a little exercise. On a scale of 1-10, with one being "very unloving," and ten being "very loving," how would you rate yourself? Enter your rating here: _____.

Now, let's read our memory verses for this chapter.

**MEMORY VERSES - 1 COR. 13:4-8**

"Love is patient, love is kind. Love does not envy, is not boastful, is not conceited, does not act improperly, is not selfish, is not provoked, and does not keep a record of wrongs. Love finds no joy in unrighteousness but rejoices in the truth. It bears all things, believes all things, hopes all things, endures all things. Love never ends. But as for prophecies, they will come to an end; as for languages, they will cease; as for knowledge, it will come to an end."

This often-quoted passage (especially at weddings) well describes *agape* love. Again, love is not merely an emotion, but a moment-by-moment decision revealing how well-connected we are with Jesus. As you go back and read the passage again, stop at each phrase and ask yourself, "Am I patient?" "Have there been moments in the last 24 hours when I have not been patient?" If you answer "yes" to that second question, then you were not being a loving person. Have you been unkind to anyone this week? If so, in those moments you weren't being a loving person.

In light of this passage, go back and rate yourself once again on a scale of 1-10, using the same standards. Enter your new rating here: _____.

If you're like me, your rating plummeted. Why is that? We recognize that we fall so short of loving perfectly. I am never completely patient. I can be unkind. So, do we just throw up our hands and quit? No, that doesn't honor Jesus. What is the issue?

We are not, in ourselves, capable of giving *agape* love. God is *agape* (1 John 4:16). Therefore, the only way for us to have and give *agape* love is for God to dwell in us through faith and bring us salvation. *Agape* is a supernatural love. We cannot manufacture this love no matter how hard we try. As an old saying goes, "You can't give what you don't have."

When Paul defines the fruit of the Spirit in Galatians 5:22, the first aspect of the fruit is *agape*. And when Jesus commands us to "*agape* your enemies" (Matt. 5:44), he knows this is an impossible command for us to obey in our flesh. Only as we live out the love of Christ are we able to accomplish true *agape* love.

When it comes to sharing the gospel, this is why Paul says in 2 Corinthians 5:14, "For Christ's love [*agape*] compels us." Notice Paul doesn't say our love compels us, but Christ's love compels us. Paul is referring to that supernatural *agape* love we only receive from Christ.

When I was a new cadet at the U.S. Military Academy, I met the Sharps, a pastor and his wife. Pastor Sharp and his wife genuinely loved cadets, especially new cadets who had just entered the academy and were in the culture shock that accompanies being a "plebe" at West Point. Their love quickly became a refuge for me. I never missed a Tuesday night gathering at the Baptist Student Union, since that is where I knew I could go and find love rather than harassment.

Jesus loved me through the Sharps. Thankfully, because of the love of Jesus through them to me and other cadets, my college years were not the typical wild and crazy college years that many experience, but years filled with growth in Christ, forging eternal friendships, and even realizing God's call on my life for ministry. It all started with the Sharps loving me with God's *agape* love.

# Questions to consider

1. Who has demonstrated *agape* love to you in your life?

2. To whom have you demonstrated *agape* love?

3. How do you differentiate between natural [*phileo*] love and supernatural [*agape*] love?

# Truths to remember

1. You can't give what you don't have. If you have not received God's *agape* love, you can't give it.

2. God's love is a supernatural reality we cannot manufacture.

# PART 7.5 | Love is the Greatest

### MEMORY VERSE - 1 COR. 13:13
"Now these three remain: faith, hope, and love. But the greatest of these is love."

In this chapter, we've seen that loving God and loving others tops the commandment list in priority. This *agape* love involves so much more than emotion. It requires will, commitment, and sacrifice. We've learned how the Scriptures show that the love of God is supernatural and cannot be humanly manufactured. Above all else, Christians are to be known by our love.

The last phrase of our memory verse, "the greatest of these is love," ought to shake us to our core. So many times, I've thought of myself as a mature Christian. After all, I've been to seminary. I've pastored churches for twenty-five years. People often comment on my proficiency in Scripture memorization and recitation. None of these pursuits or traits is bad – it's just that none of them is the greatest.

In Romans 8:28-29, Paul dumps an avalanche of theology on us when he writes:

> We know that all things work together for the good of those who love God: those who are called according to His purpose. For those He foreknew He also predestined to be conformed to the image of His Son, so that He would be the firstborn among many brothers.

Among such heavy topics as God's sovereignty and predestination, we see this amazing and hopeful truth: the "good" that God wants is for us to be conformed to the likeness of his Son.

For you and me to be conformed to the likeness of Jesus, there will always be room to grow in love. And that's the greatest means of growth available. If God is love, and Jesus is God, and Jesus is King, then love is king.

So, there's nothing more important to you and me, nothing more critical in our sanctification process, than to grow in our love for Christ and for his love to grow in us.

How do we do that? We partner with the Holy Spirit inside us and the Word of God before us. One practical method for growing in our love for Christ is to go to 1 Corinthians 13:4-8 at least once a week. As you read the passage, take out the word "love" and insert your name. So, it will look like this:

> Daniel is patient, Daniel is kind. Daniel does not envy, Daniel is not boastful, is not conceited, does not act improperly, is not selfish, is not provoked, and does not keep a record of wrongs. Daniel finds no joy in unrighteousness but rejoices in the truth. Daniel bears all things, believes all things, hopes all things, endures all things.

Even as I write this, I cringe, because every one of these statements is false. I have failed at every point this week. So, the exercise is to journal how I have failed to be patient. When was I not kind? The goal is not to beat myself up, but to preach the gospel to myself. I have sinned in each instance when I have failed to love. But Jesus died for me. He took my sin and shame. He now fills me with his Spirit to change me.

So, what patterns do you see emerge as you list the times you weren't loving? As you daily or weekly work on your "Love Better" list, let the Lord grow your awareness of the love in you and through you.

# Questions to consider

1. Why is love considered by Paul and Jesus to be the greatest?

2. How do you feel about the truth in Romans 8:28-29 that everything that happens in your life is meant to be used by God to make you more loving, like Jesus?

3. What is the most impactful truth you learned from this chapter?

# Truths to remember

1. As Christians, nothing is more important than growing in your love for Christ and him growing his love in you.

2. It's healthy for us to examine how we're loving God and others as we measure our love against Scripture.

# Memory Verses

THREE KINDS OF LOVE: "He said to him, 'Love the Lord your God with all your heart, with all your soul, and with all your mind. This is the greatest and most important command. The second is like it: Love your neighbor as yourself'" (Matt. 22:37-39).

LOVE IS A DECISION: "Love consists in this: not that we loved God, but that He loved us and sent His Son to be the propitiation for our sins" (1 John 4:10).

LOVE IS A CHRISTIAN'S TRADEMARK: "By this all people will know that you are My disciples, if you have love for one another" (John 13:35).

LOVE IS SUPERNATURAL: "Love is patient, love is kind. Love does not envy, is not boastful, is not conceited, does not act improperly, is not selfish, is not provoked, and does not keep a record of wrongs. Love finds no joy in unrighteousness but rejoices in the truth. It bears all things, believes all things, hopes all things, endures all things. Love never ends. But as for prophecies, they will come to an end; as for languages, they will cease; as for knowledge, it will come to an end" (1 Cor. 13:4-8).

LOVE IS THE GREATEST: "Now these three remain: faith, hope, and love. But the greatest of these is love" (1 Cor. 13:13).

# PART 8 | What is Forgiveness?

## By Daniel Carr

When my wife was fifteen years old, her parents divorced. Her dad had struggled with alcoholism since his teenage years, and he just refused to stop drinking. His addiction led to numerous other problems such as infidelity in the marriage.

So, my wife's parents divorced. For years, she was angry at her dad. Even after going all in with Jesus, and marrying me, and joining me in ministry, she still harbored anger, bitterness, and resentment toward her dad for breaking up the family.

About twelve years into our marriage, and deep into our ministry, the Lord convicted her of the need to forgive her dad. He hadn't sought forgiveness. He had never said he was sorry. But the Lord still made it clear she was to forgive him.

Perhaps in Christianity – and in all human life – one of the most difficult challenges is forgiving someone. Marriages are ripped apart due to a lack of forgiveness. Children become estranged from their parents due to a lack of forgiveness. Friendships are shattered due to a lack of forgiveness.

Yet even worse, without forgiveness from God, we become slaves to sin. Without forgiveness, we remain separated from God for eternity. Apart from forgiveness, there is no hope for us to have eternal life with Jesus in the most beautiful relationship imaginable.

What's so powerful about forgiveness, and why is forgiving others so hard? Why is forgiveness so important?

# PART 8.1 | Forgiveness Defined

MEMORY VERSE - JER. 31:34

"No longer will one teach his neighbor or his brother, saying, 'Know the LORD,' for they will all know Me, from the least to the greatest of them" — this is the LORD's declaration. "For I will forgive their wrongdoing and never again remember their sin."

## The beginning of a new age

On the night before Jesus was crucified, he spent hours with his disciples celebrating the Passover – the Jewish holiday in which they remembered that God faithfully led the Israelites out of Egypt in the days of Moses. The wicked Pharaoh (that's what Egyptians called their king) had refused to let the Jewish people go and had hardened his heart toward God.

So, God sent ten plagues on the land and people of Egypt, with each plague demonstrating how the Lord is the true God and not the false gods of the Egyptians. The final plague – the death of the firstborn in the land, including Pharaoh's own son – finally humbled Pharaoh so that he let God's people go.

However, God warned his people of the final plague, and instructed each household to sacrifice an unblemished male lamb and wipe some of its blood on the doorpost of the house. That night, as the death angel passed through Egypt to take the firstborn, he "passed over" the houses with blood on the doorposts and spared those inside from judgment.

As the disciples were celebrating this deliverance from judgment and slavery, Matthew 26:27-28 tells us, "Then He took a cup, and after giving thanks, He gave it to them and said, 'Drink from it, all of you. For this is My blood that establishes the covenant; it is shed for many for the forgiveness of sins.'"

We now know that Jesus was instituting the Lord's Supper, or "communion." At the time, the disciples most likely didn't realize the seriousness of this moment, but later they would understand and then establish this as an ordinance of the church. In his statement, Jesus claims this covenant – or this new age – is ratified by his blood for the forgiveness of sin. What did he mean? And what is this forgiveness?

## Definition

The Greek word often translated "forgive" has been defined as "to send forth," "send away," "let go of," "divorce."[1] So, when Scripture discusses forgiveness, the word means sending sin away, letting go of sin, or divorcing the sin from the person.

When my wife's parents were divorced, they were no longer married. They were no longer husband and wife. They weren't "together." This is what happens – in a positive light – when forgiveness takes place. The actions and adverse impact of the sinful action on the relationship are "sent away."

## Does God forget?

In Jeremiah 31:34, God says he will forgive his peoples' sins and remember them no more. Some have erroneously concluded that God "forgets" our sins. However, God is omniscient. He knows all things, therefore he does not simply forget our sin. This term in Hebrew, translated as "remembers," points to the reality that God no longer holds our sins against us. He divorces the sin from us so we are no longer bearing the weight of the punishment of our sin. How can God do that? We'll unpack the answer in the next chapter.

# Questions to consider

1. What does it look like for you to "send away" a sin someone has committed against you?

2. How does it make you feel that God separates your sin from you through forgiveness?

3. Who in your life right now are you struggling to forgive or refusing to forgive?

# Truths to remember

1. God's promise is to forgive you and no longer hold your sin against you.

2. Although God is sovereign and omniscient (he knows all things), he chooses to love us and forgive us

# PART 8.2 | The Price for Forgiveness

## MEMORY VERSE - EPH. 1:7

"We have redemption in Him through His blood, the forgiveness of our trespasses, according to the riches of His grace."

# Blood is key

It may be a gory topic, but you cannot overstate the importance of blood and sacrifice in the gospel. With the very first sin – that of Adam and Eve – we see bloodshed in order to cover sin: "The LORD God made clothing out of skins for Adam and his wife, and He clothed them" (Gen. 3:21).

To cover the nakedness, shame, and guilt of the first couple, God killed animals and made clothing from the skins for Adam and Eve. This move by God was the first act of atonement and forgiveness in Scripture, but definitely not the last. Blood is the source of life, according to Scripture: "for the blood is the life ...." (Deut. 12:23). Later, God stresses the importance of sacrifice when he says, "According to the law almost everything is purified with blood, and without the shedding of blood there is no forgiveness" (Heb. 9:22).

So, the price of forgiveness is life. The reason? Because the cost of sin is death. Paul says, "For the wages of sin is death, but the gift of God is eternal life in Christ Jesus our Lord" (Rom. 6:23).

Adam was sentenced to die because of sin, and his forgiveness cost the life of another. It's the same for us. Paul also says, "For all have sinned and fall short of the glory of God" (Rom. 3:23). All of us have sinned. Therefore, all of us are condemned to death. Our only hope of forgiveness is in the life of another, sacrificed for us.

But not just any life will do. Throughout the Old Testament, God's people sacrificed animals for that atonement. But the author of Hebrews writes, "For it is impossible for the blood of bulls and goats to take away sins" (Heb. 10:4).

So, what kind of life is required to truly take away our sins?

## Jesus, the perfect sacrifice

In Ephesians 1:7, Paul writes that our forgiveness comes through the shed blood of Jesus – his life for our sin, his blood for our forgiveness. What makes Jesus different from any other sacrifice is that he was fully human, yet sinless. He was unblemished, perfect. The Bible says, "For we do not have a high priest who is unable to sympathize with our weaknesses, but One who has been tested in every way as we are, yet without sin" (Heb. 4:15).

The price of our forgiveness is the life of God the Son – Jesus.

## Questions to consider

1. How does it make you feel to know that Jesus died as a sacrifice for you?

2. How does the fact that Jesus is God the Son add to the incredible truth of what Jesus did for us?

3. Knowing what Jesus did for you, what should your appropriate response be?

## Truths to remember

1. Our sin demands death.

2. There must be a sacrifice for life.

3. The only sufficient sacrifice is one who is perfect – God the Son, Jesus.

# PART 8.3 | Forgiveness from God

MEMORY VERSE - MARK 2:7
"Who can forgive sins but God alone?"

## Only God

Throughout biblical times, there existed an awareness that only God could forgive sins. King David, after his sins of adultery and murder, wrote to God in Psalm 51, "Against You — You alone — I have sinned and done this evil in Your sight" (Ps. 51:4).

The reason only God can forgive sins is because only God is perfect and holy. Sin cannot withstand the presence of the holy, almighty God. We see this haunting truth in the account of a man named Uzzah.

Uzzah was a son of Abinadab, a man in the priestly line of Levi. In 2 Samuel 6, we read that David was enroute to bring the Ark of the Covenant to rest in Jerusalem. The entourage came to the house of Abinadab and likely spent some time resting there. The Bible says they either built or acquired a "new cart" to transport the Ark of the Covenant.

What was the Ark of the Covenant? The ark was a golden chest God had prescribed to Moses to be one of the most holy items the Jews possessed. The ark contained the stone tablets on which God had inscribed the Ten Commandments, some of the leftover manna with which God fed his people during forty years of desert wanderings, and the staff of Moses' brother, Aaron.

Yet, even more critical than what the ark contained was what the ark represented. The Ark of the Covenant represented the very presence of God with his people. When they went into battle, they were to carry the ark before them. Once per year, the high priest would offer the annual sacrifice on the Day of Atonement and sprinkle the blood onto the lid of the Ark of the Covenant, called the Mercy Seat. The Ark of the Covenant manifested the presence of God. Therefore, the Ark of the Covenant was holy, as God is holy.

When King David and his group were ready to leave the house of Abinadab, they placed the ark on the new cart. Uzzah was one of the young men assigned to walk alongside the cart to ensure the ark's safe travel. However, in 2 Samuel 6:6, we read that the oxen pulling the cart stumbled. Uzzah reached out his hand to steady the ark. When he did, the Bible says, "God struck him dead on the spot for his irreverence, and he died there next to the ark of God" (v. 7).

When the normal, sinful human Uzzah came into personal contact with the holiness of God, he died. Uzzah made the mistake of thinking his hand was more worthy than the ground God created. Being in the priestly tribe, Uzzah would have been aware of the laws concerning the handling of the Ark of the Covenant. Yet, he neglected those laws. And, since sin cannot withstand the holiness of God, he died.

# Our dilemma

Our dilemma is the same as Uzzah's. We're sinners, and we're not able to withstand the presence of the holy God of the universe. The prophet Isaiah says, "But your iniquities have built barriers between you and your God, and your sins have made Him hide His face from you so that He does not listen" (Isa. 59:2).

Even beyond separating us from God, our sins have placed us at enmity with God. We see in the word "enmity" the word "enemy." Paul writes, "the carnal mind is enmity against God" (Rom. 8:7 KJV). Before we're saved, all we have is a carnal mind. The word "carnal" means "of the flesh." So, not only are we separated from God, we actually oppose him. Even worse, there's nothing we can do about it on our own. We're not able to earn our forgiveness.

Somehow, we must be reconciled to God. Somehow, we must be forgiven by God himself. But how? The answer is Jesus.

# Questions to consider

1. How have you sinned against God this week?

2. What do you think about when you read that, at one time, you were at enmity with God?

3. What does it mean that God is holy?

# Truths to remember

1. God is holy, and sin cannot withstand the presence of God.

2. Only God can forgive sins.

# PART 8.4 | Forgiveness through Christ

### MEMORY VERSES - COL. 2:12-14

"Having been buried with Him in baptism, you were also raised with Him through faith in the working of God, who raised Him from the dead. And when you were dead in trespasses and in the uncircumcision of your flesh, He made you alive with Him and forgave us all our trespasses. He erased the certificate of debt, with its obligations, that was against us and opposed to us, and has taken it out of the way by nailing it to the cross."

## The love of God

Only God can forgive our sins. Only he can restore us to a right relationship with him. God the Son, Jesus, came to earth to accomplish this restoration. But why would God want to reconcile us to himself? Why would he want to save those who were at enmity with him?

The answer is love. God loves us. He loves you. "For God loved the world in this way: He gave His One and Only Son, so that everyone who believes in Him will not perish but have eternal life" (John 3:16). God knew our dilemma. He is just; therefore our sin demands punishment. Yet, he still loves us as our creator and ruler of the universe.

So, God solved our problem for us. God the Son came because he loves us. God's love for you is constant and unconditional. There's never been a time, nor will there ever be a time, when God loves you more than he does right now.

## The power of the cross

In the passage from Colossians cited above, we see all that Jesus accomplished for us through his sacrifice on the cross. He brings to life believers who once were spiritually dead (which is all of mankind). He reconciles us to himself so that we now have the peace of God and peace with God. But also, as we read, he forgives us all our trespasses. That is, God forgives all our sins.

Wow! Just think about that. How many times in the past week did you get angry at someone and think about retaliation? How about lust? How about physical sins? Sexual sins? Jealousy? Envy? Greed? Gluttony? Dishonesty? Ouch!

Yet, in Jesus, we're totally forgiven. Not because we've earned it or because we get better and better. We're totally forgiven because that's how powerful Jesus' sacrifice for us is. All our sins are forgiven – the past ones, the present ones, and even the future ones. There truly is power in the blood.

# Sent away

When you and I place our trust in Jesus, he forgives us. He separates our sin from us. He remembers our sin no more in that he no longer holds our sin against us. The psalmist writes, "As far as the east is from the west, so far has He removed our transgressions from us" (Ps. 103:12). To "forgive" is to send away or divorce. Because of Jesus, we are divorced from our sins. Jesus already paid the price owed.

When Jesus was on the cross, the Bible records seven statements he made. One of these is translated, "It is finished!" (John 19:30). This was a common phrase in Greek. When someone made a final payment on a debt, his loan certificate would be stamped with the Greek word *tetelestai*, "paid in full." This is what Jesus yelled out from the cross. Our sins are forgiven. They are paid in full. That is the power and the glory of the cross for you and me. Jesus paid it all!

# Questions to consider

1. How good does it feel when (or if) your debt is totally cleared out?

2. What does it mean for God to forgive you?

3. Knowing that God loves you unconditionally, how should you live in response to that?

# Truths to remember

1. Jesus paid for all your sins – every single one of them.

2. When you trust in Christ, God sends your guilt away.

3. Your forgiveness includes your future sins.

# PART 8.5 | Forgiving Others

## Ph.D.-level Christianity

In this deep dive into forgiveness, we've discussed God's forgiveness of you and me. What a liberating and deeply moving truth! But also, the truth of the gospel, and the forgiveness we receive, change us so that we are to live a different way. What is that way? Well, it includes our hearts and willingness to forgive others. This isn't easy. In fact, apart from Jesus, it's impossible.

Jesus says, "For if you forgive people their wrongdoing, your heavenly Father will forgive you as well. But if you don't forgive people, your Father will not forgive your wrongdoing" (Matt. 6:14-15).

What does Jesus mean by this? Forgiving others is proof you have been born again and forgiven by God. To forgive someone takes the power and love of God in us to accomplish. If you're not born again, you don't have the Spirit of God dwelling in you to empower you to do this nearly impossible feat. Paul reminds us, "For it is God who is working in you, enabling you both to desire and to work out His good purpose" (Phil. 2:13).

## How do I forgive someone?

To forgive someone who has deeply wronged you is perhaps the most difficult act anyone can do. Forgiveness is selfless. Forgiveness is almost always undeserved. We are called to forgive others in spite of their actions – even if they don't ask to be forgiven. But what does that process look like? Is it automatic? Is it immediate? The answer to these questions is a resounding "no."

Looking at Ephesians 4:32, God gives us a blueprint for the forgiveness process. So, let's look at this, one step at a time. To start, let's look at the end of the verse.

1. **JUST AS GOD ALSO FORGAVE YOU IN CHRIST.** You won't be able to forgive someone unless you have personally experienced God's forgiveness through Jesus. Have you trusted in Christ as Lord? Have you turned from your sinful pursuits and begun to pursue Jesus?

2. **BE KIND TO ONE ANOTHER.** This is where the process of forgiving others begins. Be kind. Don't retaliate. Don't try to get even. Don't try to make them "pay" in some way. You may not feel like being kind to them; your emotions may be raging. Yet, those who walk in the Spirit manifest the fruit of the Spirit – love, joy, peace, kindness, faithfulness, gentleness, goodness, and self-control. It's okay to be kind when you don't feel like it. It doesn't mean you're a hypocrite. You're exercising self-control. Be kind!

3. **BE COMPASSIONATE.** Once you're being kind, it's time to work on your heart. Let your heart soften towards others. We cannot overemphasize the importance of this step. Try to place yourself in their shoes. What's going on in their lives? What kinds of stresses are they under? When you place yourself in their shoes, your understanding of why they act as they do becomes clearer. This doesn't mean their sin is okay. It's not. But being tenderhearted helps you move in the direction of forgiving them.

4. **FORGIVE THEM.** Send their sin away. Divorce what they did to you from them. Hold it against them no more. Paul writes here that the model for forgiving someone is the way Jesus forgave us. He sent our sin away. He holds our sin against us no more. He loves unconditionally.

5. **LET THEM REBUILD TRUST.** Forgiving someone does not mean you automatically trust them again. To do so would often be foolish. However, forgiving them does mean you open yourself up to them so that, over time, they can regain your trust.

# Questions to consider

1. Who do you need to forgive?

2. What steps have you taken to forgive others?

3. What is your next step?

# Truths to remember

1. We aren't able to truly forgive someone unless we have personally experienced the forgiveness of God in our lives.

2. God commands us to forgive others. It's not an option.

3. God empowers us to forgive others.

4. Forgiveness is a biblical process.

# Memory Verses

**FORGIVENESS DEFINED:** "No longer will one teach his neighbor or his brother, saying, 'Know the LORD,' for they will all know Me, from the least to the greatest of them" — this is the LORD'S declaration. "For I will forgive their wrongdoing and never again remember their sin" (Jer. 31:34).

**THE PRICE FOR FORGIVENESS:** "We have redemption in Him through His blood, the forgiveness of our trespasses, according to the riches of His grace" (Eph. 1:7).

**FORGIVENESS FROM GOD:** "Who can forgive sins but God alone?" (Mark 2:7).

**FORGIVENESS THROUGH CHRIST:** "And when you were dead in trespasses and in the uncircumcision of your flesh, He made you alive with Him and forgave us all our trespasses. He erased the certificate of debt, with its obligations, that was against us and opposed to us, and has taken it out of the way by nailing it to the cross" (Col. 2:13-14).

**FORGIVING OTHERS:** "And be kind and compassionate to one another, forgiving one another, just as God also forgave you in Christ" (Eph. 4:32).

# Notes

## PART 1: WHO IS GOD?

1. James R. White, *The Forgotten Trinity*, (Minneapolis: Bethany House Publishers, 1998), 26.

2. Ibid.

3. Graphic found at https://tmrichmond3.net/2014/07/02/the-trinity-not-quite-explained/trinity-graphic/.

4. White, 27.

5. Phillip Schaff, *The Creeds of Christendom*, Vol. 2 (Grand Rapids, MI: Baker Books, 1931), 57-58.

6. A. W. Tozer, *The Knowledge of the Holy* (New York: Harper Collins Publishers, 1961), 1.

7. White, 139.

## PART 2: WHAT IS CONFESSION OF SIN?

1. C. S. Lewis, *The Magician's Nephew* (New York: Harper Collins, 1994), 126.

## PART 3: WHAT IS REPENTANCE?

1. Thomas Watson, *The Doctrine of Repentance* (United Kingdom: Banner of Truth, n.d.), 30.

2. John Piper, https://www.desiringgod.org/messages/battling-the-unbelief-of-misplaced-shame.

3. J. Scott Duvall, *Devotions on the Greek New Testament* (Grand Rapids, MI: Zondervan Academic, 2012), 47.

4. John Newton, *From Disgrace to Amazing Grace* (Wheaton, IL: Crossway, 2007), 149.

## PART 4: WHAT IS JUSTIFICATION?

1. https://www.gbtseminary.org/cheap-grace-bonhoeffer-and-the-cost-of-discipleship/.

2. https://www.wholesomewords.org/poetry/crosby2.html.

## PART 5: WHAT IS FAITH?

1. https://rcus.org/confessions-2/.

2. https://ses.edu/minimal-facts-on-the-resurrection-that-even-skeptics-accept/.

3. R. C. Sproul, *Faith Alone: The Evangelical Doctrine of Justification* (Grand Rapids, MI: Baker Books, 2017), 156.

## PART 6: WHAT IS PRAYER?

1. C. S. Lewis, "C. S. Lewis Quotes on Prayer," found at https://lifearoundthetable.ca/c-s-lewis-quotes-on-prayer/#:~:text=I%20pray%20because%20I%20can,It%20doesn't%20change%20God.

## PART 7: WHAT IS LOVE?

1. "Americans less likely to partner up and get married," https://www.wbaltv.com/article/americans-partnership-marriage-survey/39078706#.

2. "What Is Eros Love?" https://www.learnreligions.com/what-is-eros-love-700682.

3. *Thayer's Greek Lexicon*, PC Study Bible, formatted electronic database, Biblesoft, Inc., 2006.

4. *Abbott-Smith Manual Greek Lexicon of the New Testament*, PC Study Bible, formatted electronic database, Biblesoft, Inc., 2014.

## PART 8: WHAT IS FORGIVENESS?

1. *Abbott-Smith Manual Greek Lexicon of the New Testament*.

# About the Authors

**DANIEL CARR** has served as lead pastor of Canaan Baptist Church in St. Louis since 2012. Daniel is a graduate of Southern Baptist Theological Seminary and the United States Military Academy. He is married to Tara, and they have seven children.

**BRAD DELAUGHTER** is lead pastor of First Baptist Church, De Soto, Missouri. Brad also serves as leader for the Missouri team of the Prison Seminaries Foundation and an adjunct professor at New Orleans Baptist Theological Seminary (NOBTS). He also holds a Ph.D. from NOBTS. Brad is married to Kristin, and they have four children.

**MARTIN WINSLOW** has served as pastor of families and missions for Canaan Baptist Church in St. Louis since 2017. Martin is a graduate of Midwestern Baptist Theological Seminary. Martin and his wife, Amy, have five children.

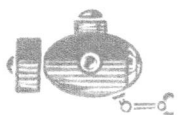

Made in the USA
Monee, IL
07 August 2023

40612163R00109